REELFOOT LAKE REMEMBERED

by

Russell H. Caldwell

First Printing: July, 2005
Printed in China

ISBN: 0-9623039-7-6
Library of Congress Control Number: 2005906814

Published by Caldwell's Office Outfitters, Inc.
P. O. Box 99
Union City, Tennessee, 38281 USA

Magic Hole
Photograph by Robert E. Clendenin, Jr.

DEDICATION

To Donna, my special lady,
my wife . . .
without whose love, help and
encouragement
this book could not have been written.

Dr. William F. "Chubby" Andrews

FOREWORD

One day, more than twenty years ago, Russell Caldwell gave me a special tour of the environs of Reelfoot, TN, including much of Reelfoot Lake itself. I was infatuated with his vast knowledge of Reelfoot, completely encompassing the people that surround the lake, many of whom earn their living as did their ancestors by fishing, hunting and guiding on these premises. I was so amazed and interested in what he had to say that I turned to him and said, "Russ, you should write a book about the things that you have told me; the story of Reelfoot boats, the oar locks that enable one to see where he is going when paddling one of these incredible little boats, the Reelfoot guides and the many men that have made now famous collectible duck calls and decoys." These things just rolled off his tongue in a constant stream, holding me spellbound.

Russell took my advice and an enlightening book soon came to fruition, and I was privileged to write the foreword in that fine book.

Nearly 20 years have passed and my friendship with Russell has grown as we have spent hundreds of hours on this unique lake formed by our great God in that terrible earthquake of 1811 and 1812. Many changes have taken place on the lake and many changes have taken place in Russell's life and my life as well. Russell's love for Reelfoot has grown deeper from year to year and his knowledge has grown as well. He is now the owner of an unusually fine duck call collection that contains calls of nearly every man living and dead that enjoyed the sport of duck hunting and the art of making and using duck calls. He has grown to be one of the finest shots that I have ever hunted with, and I would class him as coequal to my great friend Nash Buckingham, recognized as one of the finest shots of the past century. His son Rob is right there with him, especially in bringing down "The Hi-Uns."

Russ wants more and more people to appreciate the amenities of Reelfoot Lake and to have a deeper knowledge and appreciation that this great body of water affords. Therefore, he has abandoned himself to a new book on Reelfoot with many more pictures, many more stories and numerous remarks from people whose lives have been lived on the lake and its premises.

I know it is going to be a best seller because it has taken shape in the heart of a man that burns with enthusiasm and love like no other man, having spent years with his father Chester Caldwell along as guide, fish cleaner and jack of all trades, and with his son Rob relishing every moment out there on the lake.

So I give you the best from the pen of a man that loves Reelfoot Lake more than any other.

With Great Affection,
Dr. William F. "Chubby" Andrews

TABLE OF CONTENTS

Photograph by Donna Caldwell

INTRODUCTION

It's been eighteen years since my first book about Reelfoot Lake and I have added many more sunrises and sunsets to my memories of this wonderful place. This new book is totally rewritten except for the History of Reelfoot and a few of the stories. It includes new pictures, most of them in color and some great old Sabin black and whites. There is a new section on the clubs on the lake and a section on the guides and top shots that hunted and fished on the lake.

The duck call section has been totally redone with great pictures and information featuring the call makers who did the best work and had the most impact on the call making craft. I am also including several contemporary callmakers that have started making calls in the Reelfoot area since the last book in 1989.

The later sections of the book are totally different; they are written with the hope they will make a difference in peoples' lives. I have used essays, quotes, poems, stories and thoughts of friends, family and other writers to bring some special things together in hope of giving the reader a vision of what the possibilities are for a happy, successful life.

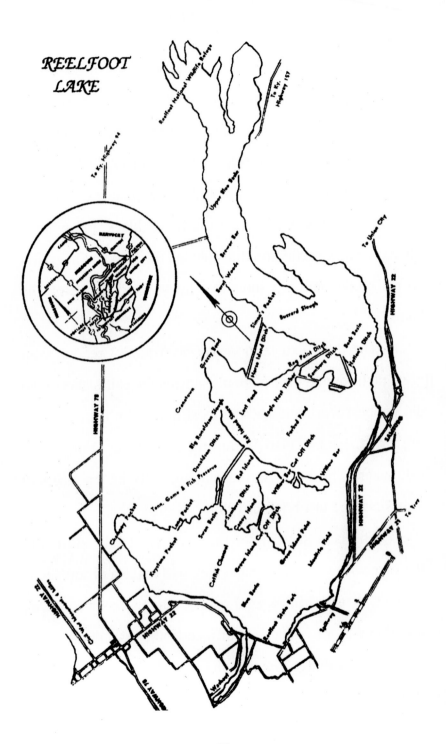

REELFOOT
LAKE

Photograph by Vern Sabin

THE HISTORY

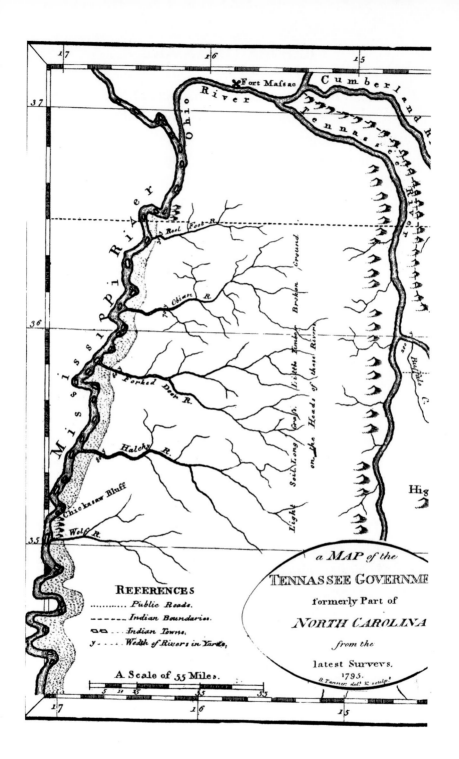

a MAP of the
TENNASSEE GOVERNME
formerly Part of
NORTH CAROLINA
from the
latest Surveys.
1795.
R Tanner del. K soulp.

REFERENCES
.... Public Roads.
- - - - - Indian Boundaries.
◠◡ - - Indian Towns.
y - - - - Width of Rivers in Yards,

A Scale of 55 Miles.

BEFORE THE QUAKE

Years before the Reelfoot happening, the Northwest Tennessee area was the home of the Paleo-Indian tribes. Afterward (approximately 500 B.C.) Woodland Indians, noted for their huge burial mounds, settled in the West Tennessee and Missouri area on both sides of the Mississippi River. These Indians built huge temple mounds on top of each other, sometimes to a height of fifteen feet.

The next Indians on the land were the early Mississipian Indians. They added to the previous mounds and built others in the lake area, extending their territory further north into West Kentucky and Southern Illinois. Many of their smaller mounds are still visible today on the islands out in Reelfoot Lake and on the northwest side of the lake.

The Chickasaw claimed all of the West Tennessee area in time, and signs of their culture are still evident. These Indians occupied the area until the time of the first white men to come through as explorers and hunters.

The first recorded white man to look on the West Tennessee area was the explorer Hernando DeSoto and his band of soldiers who came up the Mississippi River in 1541. Having crossed the "Great River" as he called the Mississippi, his expedition continued north along the west side of the river through Arkansas and into Missouri. As they hiked north, the party had to wade through mud and swamps. In time, they came upon the district of Little Prairie (Caruthersville), and the high, dry lands which extend toward New Madrid. Here religions of the natives and their invaders came into contact. DeSoto had his men erect a large cross on a mound by the river. Mass was celebrated with much ceremony, with kneeling soldiers and Indians present. Historians believe this to have been the first Christian service to be held west of the Mississippi and the site used for the ceremony could have been a large Indian mound near New Madrid. From this elevation, DeSoto could have viewed Madrid Bend and Lake County.

DeSoto died of fever in 1542. Fearing attack by the Indians, the Spaniards buried DeSoto in the river he called "The Father of Waters," ending his dream of riches he thought the area held. A few of his men survived the seven hundred mile trip down river after much sickness and many Indian battles, to return to Spain and there to write and tell of their adventures.

In 1566 and 1567 Juan Pardo, also a Spaniard, led another expedition west in search of gold. During his travels he had numerous wars with the Indians of Tennessee and he built the first forts in the area now known as Tennessee. The forts were soon abandoned and the Spaniards moved east to return to Spain.

To keep the English from claiming the Misssissippi Valley, the French government sent Jacques Marquette and Louis Joliet south from Canada in 1672 and 1673 to claim the area for France. Marquette notes in his journal going as far south on the Mississippi River as the Arkansas River, then they reversed their trip and passed the Lake County shore going both ways. Marquette marveled at the canebrakes and buffaloes on both sides of the river in the area. It is thought that the exploration party landed to meet with an Indian tribe in the Reelfoot/Lake County area because of his map showing an area similar to the Hickman Bluffs and the Reelfoot River and Obion River as described in his journal and maps.

In 1682 another French expedition under the command of Robert Cavalier de la Salle and Lieutenant Henry Tonty traveled from Illinois country to the Gulf of Mexico. In Tonty's journal there is a paragraph relating to Lake County. It reads as follows:

Continuing our journey, we come...to a river called by the Iroquois "Oyo" [Ohio]...Finally passing through forty leagues in an inundated country, with lodges here and there upon the banks [occupied by the Chickasaw], we reached a hill where we encamped to hunt; but the place being unsuitable, we descended three leagues further."

In 1699 Father St. Cosme and in 1700 Father Gravier passed the same way on missionary journeys. Father St. Cosme noted in his journal the pre-earthquake signs that the earth trembled violently enough for all to perceive. This corroborates the statement that earthquakes had been felt in the area before the big quake.

Not until 1785 did the white men come into the West Tennessee area to stay for any length of time. Henry Rutherford, with companions Alex and Amos Moore came from North Carolina by river to survey. They named one of the rivers where they camped, the Forked Deer. They started their survey of the area at a point west of Ripley known as Key Corner, and all West Tennessee Surveys since have used that as a reference point. Three years later Henry Rutherford was surveying in the Lake County section. Here one of his helpers, James Carleton, made a survey called the "I. C. Line." This line is the main street of Tiptonville today.

Tennessee became a state in 1796, but West Tennessee was not added until 1818. Andrew Jackson paid the Chickasaws $15,000 per year for twenty years, to purchase a territory of over six million acres at a cost of five cents per acre. This purchase included all land west of the Tennessee River and south of the Ohio River to the Mississippi-Alabama line.

The first white landowner in the Reelfoot Lake area was a Revolutionary War soldier named George Doherty, who was deeded 4,800 acres in Tennessee for military service in the Continental Line by North Carolina. He purchased from the state an additional 12,000 acres in the northwest corner of the state as a land speculation. This acreage was a heavily wooded land, irrigated by what is now known as Reelfoot Creek and Bayou DuChien.

Sir Charles Lyell, author of "Principles of Geology", stated after he visited the United States in 1854, that the Indians told of the earthquakes which had previously devastated this area. This has been confirmed many times by geologic evidence. Faulting in rocks of the area indicate that the earthquakes had occurred in the area for several thousand years. Historian Myron Fuller found old bayous sunk by prior earthquakes with trees growing in them several hundred years old. Part of the Tiptonville Dome was uplifted before 1811 and Fuller found cracks with trees fully two hundred years old growing in their bottom, indicating earlier quakes of severe intensity.

Prior to 1811, not only were there shocks to foretell of the coming disaster, but the animals left the area in droves. Thousands of squirrels perished in the Ohio River in the days before the quake, and stories are told of other animals fleeing south before the December 16 event.

Photograph by Vern Sabin
Looking south from Samburg

THE LEGEND OF REELFOOT

There is an interesting legend told, with several variations, about the formation of Reelfoot Lake:

At the beginning of the nineteenth century in the rich bottom lands along the east banks of the Mississippi dwelt a tribe of the Chickasaws. At the time of our story, a mighty chief ruled the tribe wisely yet with deep unhappiness, for his only son had been born with a deformed foot. When the boy grew up, he walked and ran with a rolling motion so his people called him Kalopin, meaning "Reelfoot."

At the death of his father, Reelfoot became chief of his people. The young chief was sad and lonely, for none of the Indian maidens stirred in him the thoughts of love. He had often heard tales of a mighty tribe, with many beautiful maidens, that lived in the south. One spring he gathered a few of his chosen warriors and wandered south in quest of a princess for his wife.

Reelfoot journeyed many days and finally approached the village of the great Choctaw chief, Copiah. When the village was reached, Reelfoot went foward to offer the required homage to Copiah. Then, the legend continues, he beheld his dream princess, the daughter of Copiah, sitting beside the chief.

Reelfoot asked Copiah for his daughter in marriage, but the old chief did not want his daughter to marry a cripple, even though he might be a powerful chieftain. Therefore, he told Reelfoot that his daughter was to be given in wedlock only to a Choctaw chieftain. Sick at heart, young Reelfoot was but more firmly resolved to have this one Indian maiden.

He offered her father many treasures, but the old Chief sent for the tribe's medicine man to call publicly on the Great Spirit.

The Great Spirit spoke to Reelfoot, saying that an Indian must not steal a wife from a neighboring tribe and that if he disobeyed and carried off the princess, the Great Spirit would cause the earth to rock and the waters to swallow up his village and bury his people in a watery grave.

Frightened by this threat, Reelfoot returned home with a heavy heart. He spent the summer helping his people gather their food for the winter, but he could not keep from thinking of his love and wondering if the Great Spirit would do as he said. For the first time, Reelfoot did not want to believe the Great Spirit; then as the days grew short, he made plans with his warriors to go south and capture the forbidden maiden. When the first snows came, Reelfoot and his men swooped down upon the Choctaws, seized the princess, and fled back to the north.

When the young chief returned with his princess, there was a great rejoicing among his people, for now their tribal family was complete. The festive fires burned; the pots boiled and venison browned on the spit. But lo, in the midst of the festivities and marriage rites, the earth began to roll. The Indians tried to flee to the hills, but the rocking earth made them reel and stagger as the Great Spirit stamped his foot in anger. The Father of Waters heard, and backing on his course, rushed over and covered Reelfoot's country. Where the Great Spirit stamped his foot, the Mississippi formed a beautiful lake, in the bottom of which lay buried Reelfoot, his bride, and his people.

Great Blue Herron with duck flushing off water
Photograph courtesy of Albert Markham

THE EARTHQUAKE

What happened on the morning of December 16th is best told by eyewitness accounts. The most famous of these accounts was written in 1826 by New Madrid resident Eliza Bryan to the Reverend Lorenzo Dow:

> Dear Brother: I have just received your kind letter, written some three or four weeks ago, requesting me to give you a description of the late horrible visitation of Providence, and the sinking of Reelfoot Lake in this section.
>
> The morning of December 15, 1811, was cloudy and a dense fog prevailed, and towards nightfall the heavens showed signs of distress. On the following morning, the 16th, about five o'clock a.m., we felt the shock of an earthquake, accompanied by a rumbling noise resembling the distant firing of a cannon, which was followed in a few minutes by the complete saturation of the atmosphere with sulphurous vapor. The moon was shining brilliantly, but the sulphurous vapor caused the earth to be wrapped in absolute darkness. The wailing inhabitants, the stampede of fowls and beasts, the noise of falling timber, the roaring of the Mississippi -- the current of which was retrograde for a few minutes -- formed a scene too appalling to conceive of. Then until daylight a number of lighter shocks occurred, one that was more violent and severe than the first one, and the terror which prevailed after the first shock was now even worse than before. The people fled hither and yon, supposing that there was less danger at a distance from the

river which was boiling, foaming and roaring terrifically. Men, women and children gave up in despair, some praying and others fainting, so great was their fear.

There were light shocks each day until January 23, 1812, when one as hard as the first occurred, followed by the same phenomena. From this time until February 4th the earth was in continual agitation, visibly waving as a gentle sea. That day a shock, almost as severe as the others, occurred, and on the 8th, about sunrise, a concussion took place, so much more violent than the others that it was called "the hard shock". The earth was transformed into total darkness, the chickens went back to roost, the cows mooed and the frightened horses pitifully neighed. At first the Mississippi River seemed to recede from its banks, and its waters, gathering up like a mountain, leaving for a short period of time many boats which were passing down the river, on the bottom of the river, during which time the crews escaped to land in safety. The river rose ten to fifteen feet perpendicularly, expanding, as it were, at the same time the banks were overflowed with a retrograde current. The river falling immediately, receded within its banks again with such violence that it took with it whole groves of young cottonwood trees and much cattle and stock.

A great many fish were left on the banks, being unable to keep up with the water, and an old canoe, antique in construction was washed ashore. The river was a mass of floating wrecks of boats, and it is said that one was wrecked in which there was a lady and six children, all of whom were lost.

In the hard shocks described, the earth was horribly lacerated -- the surface from time to time was covered over of uneven depths by the sand which issued from the fissures, which were made in great numbers all over the country, some of which closed up immediately after they had vomited forth their sand and water. In many places, however, there was a substance resembling coal thrown up with the sand. It is impossible to say what the depth of the fissures or irregular breaks were. The site of New Madrid, Missouri, was settled down at least fifteen feet, and not more than half a mile below that town there does not appear to be any alteration of the river, but back from the river a short distance the numerous large ponds or lakes, which covered a great part of the country, were totally dried up. The beds of some of them bulged above their former banks several feet.

The most remarkable feature of all the entire disturbances, which was not generally known for some months afterwards, was the discovery of a huge lake on the Tennessee side of the Mississippi River, upwards of 25 miles long and from one-half to eight miles in width. This lake was later called Reelfoot Lake. There are places in it the bottom of which has never been found, though many efforts have been made to ascertain the depth of these places.

The lake has communication with the Mississippi River at both ends, and it is conjectured that it will not be many years before the principal part, if not the whole of the Mississippi will pass that way. In the last year or so an herb, resembling moss, has literally covered the surface or the lake, and during the winter months wild fowls, such as ducks, geese, cranes, etc., winter on the lake and eat this moss as food. Deer and other animals seem to enjoy it.

It is said that where the lake was formed was a vast area of fine timbered lands, and in places only the tops of trees can be seen. The lake runs north and south, and each end has a neck shape, widening out about the center, or nearer the northern terminus than the center. The water in it does not seem to rise or lower to any marked degree, and the lake is destined to become the great hunting and fishing resort of the west.

It is said that where this lake was formed was formerly the Indians' hunting grounds, and also where they held their annual war dances; but since the terrible visitation of the earthquake it is a rare thing that one ventures in that vicinity. By some method, known only to themselves, they marked a warning on the trees for other Indians to keep away. Most of those who fled from the vicinity during the hard shocks returned, but always greatly alarmed at the slightest trembling of the earth. We have, since their commencement in 1811,...felt light shocks. Hardly a week passes but we feel one. There were two the past winter, much more severe than we have felt them for several years before. Since then, however, they are lighter than ever, and as the months and years pass the inhabitants are becoming more and more reconciled to the surroundings.

One circumstance worthy of mention is: This section was once subject to severe thunder, but for a long time previous to the first shocks there was no thunder at all and but very little since.

Respectfully yours,
E. Bryan
New Madrid, MO

Another unusually interesting account of the second quake (in February) is given by Vincent Nolte, a famous German merchant. Mr. Nolte was on the river at the time, bringing a barge down on the way to the Gulf of Mexico. His description is given here as translated from the original account in German.

The Ohio had been frozen over for several days and for more than a week past no boat had descended the stream; hence my boats and my friend Hollander's were frozen up on the way between Limestone and Louisville. Three days afterwards, just as we had all sat down to dinner, the whole house was violently shaken; glasses, plants, and bottles jingled and fell from the board; most of the guests leaped to their feet exclaiming "here is the earthquake, by jingo! there is no humbug about it!" as they rushed out into the street. But all was still again and everyone gradually returned to his house. Early the next morning I learned that the earthquake had loosened the ice from the Ohio and had again opened the current of the stream and that several boats, among others two flatboats fastened together had been carried down over the Falls lying between Louisville and the little town of Shippingport, situated at a distance of a few miles from the former place. I at once rode over to Shippingport and found my boats and companions in safety. So soon as we had replenished and increased our stock of provisions I returned to my boats, and having recommenced our journey, we in a few days left the clear transparent waters of the Ohio and passed by its junction with the mighty Mississippi into the thick and turbid flood of the latter stream. We floated on quietly for several days, arresting our course as was usual at night, and securing our boats in any way we could to the river bank. In flat boats like ours, it is a rule never to trust your boat in the night to the force of the current, for the surface of the water is so broken by trees which have been swept away from the shore and then became fast imbedded in the bottom of the river where they remain immovable and are designated by the names of "planters," as well as those which are likewise imbedded but which have an up and down motion whence they are known by the title of "sawyers,"that it is an impossibility to avoid them at night, and in fact to do so is difficult in broad daylight. In this way we reached the small town of New Madrid, on the 6th day of February. Some twenty boats which had left Shippingport at the same time with us kept us company.

It was a clear moonlight night; my friend Hollander had retired to rest and I was sitting about twelve o'clock at a little table sketching a caricature of Madison, the President of the United States and of whom it was said he was under a petticoat government.

I had just given the last touches to a somewhat dilapidated red house when there came a frightful crash like the sudden explosion of artillery and instantly followed by countless flashes of lightning; the Mississippi foamed up like the water in a boiling cauldron and the stream flowed rushing back, while the trees, near which we lay, came crashing and thundering down. This fearful spectacle lasted for several minutes; and the fierce flashes of lightning, the rush of the receding waters, and the crash of falling trees seemed as if they would never end.

Hollander, starting halfway up in bed, hurriedly exclaimed, "What is that, Nolte?" What other answer could I give him but that I myself did not know, yet supposed it to be the effect of an earthquake. I clamored up to the roof of our boat. What a spectacle! Our flats were indeed still floating, but far away from the shore where we had moored them at nightfall. The agitated water all about us, full of trees and branches, which the stream now flowing in its proper current was rapidly sweeping away, and a light only here and there visible from the town-in short a real chaos.

The feeble crew which I had brought along with me from Pittsburgh to man my flatboats, consisted of three sailors whom want of employment at the seaports while the "Embargo" lasted had driven them to the inland city and a river pilot acquainted with those streams. They told me that the boats around us had let go the tackle which secured them to the shore and were now floating down the stream, and asking whether we had not better do the same thing.

I at once reflected that if under the circumstances, it was dangerous and by no means advisable to trust to the stream in the night, it must be now much more so, when the danger was greatly increased by the trees which the earthquake had loosened and driven away, and then consequently it would be better to remain where we were until daylight had returned and we could see our way.

At sunrise the whole terrible scene was disclosed to our gaze. The little town of New Madrid sunken, destroyed, and overflowed to three-fourths of its extent, lay more than five hundred paces from us with some of its scattered inhabitants here and there visible among the ruins.

Our boats were fixed in the middle of an island formed by fallen trees, and several hours passed before the crew could cut a passage for them and get out. At length we were again floating on the stream and continued our course by day's journeys until we arrived on the thirty-second day after our departure from Pittsburgh in Natchez in the State of Mississippi. Here we heard all kind of details concerning the earthquake as it had been noticed in that place. We remained a week during which time not a single one of the boats arrived which had surrounded us on the evening of the 6th of February.

When we reached New Orleans we learned that the earthquake had not been any further perceptible there than that the chandeliers in the ballroom had all at once been observed to rock from side to side, and that a number of ladies had felt quite ill while others instantly fainted.

This remarkable earthquake which was so disastrous in its consequences commenced in the Northwestern part of the State of Missouri, shook the whole extent of Louisiana, more or less, and stretched throughout the whole region lying around the Gulf of Mexico as far as Caracus, Venezuela, where it finally raged with terrible fury almost entirely destroying that town itself and reducing to poverty or swallowing up 40,000 inhabitants there and in several other places in the neighborhood.

Of the boats which surrounded us on the evening of February 6th, nothing was ever afterwards heard and we probably would have shared the same fate had it not been for the plan we adopted of remaining by the shore.

These observations of the formation of Reelfoot Lake are valuable and interesting, since they consist of the most reliable written accounts by eyewitnesses of the earthquake, from which we may make a comparison of this phenomena.

Reelfoot was not the only lake formed by the quake; there were several lakes in eastern Arkansas, as well as Caddo Lake on the Louisiana border, which I visited in the 1970's. It looks exactly like Reelfoot, except it is smaller in size. It is stump filled, full of sloughs and cypress trees.

The rolling motion of the earth is illustrated (when flying over the lake in a plane) by the parallel lines of cypress trees growing on the ridges in the bottom of the Lake. Early pictures show the trees so thick you couldn't see across the Lake. Later, after 1860, a great forest fire razed through the area and turned most of the trees into the stumps we now see.

One of the most graphic descriptions of the destruction left by the earthquake was by Timothy Flint describing the Caruthersville community in his book, The Travels of Timothy Flint.

They had their settlement, which consisted of 100 families and which was located in a wide and very deep and fertile bottom, broken up. When I passed it and stopped to contemplate the traces of the catastrophe which remained after seven years, the crevices where the earth had burst were sufficiently manifest, and the whole region was covered with sand to a depth of two or three feet.

The surface was red with oxided pyrites of iron, and the sand blows, as they were called, were abundantly mixed with this kind of earth and with pieces of pit coal. But two families remained of the whole settlement...When I resided there, this district, formerly so level, rich and beautiful, had the most melancholy of all aspects of decay, the tokens of former cultivation and habitancy, which were now mementos of desolation and destruction.

Large and beautiful orchards left uninclosed, houses uninhabited, deep chasms in the earth obvious at frequent intervals. Such was the face of the country, although the people had for years become so accustomed to frequent and small shocks, which did no essential injury, that the lands were gradually rising again in value, and New Madrid was slowly rebuilding with frail buildings adapted to the apprehensions of the people.

Some interesting causes of the formation of the lake have been revealed upon examination. The surface soil was layer upon layer of loose sand and clay to a depth of two thousand feet. The makeup of this soil was caused by prior earthquakes and the continued shifting of the Mississippi River over its floodplain. Some earlier writers mention the extrusion of sand along the lower part of Reelfoot Creek in amounts that would clog the channel and obstruct draining and increase the ponding opportunity. The land on the south end of the lake is about ten to fifteen feet above the lake, creating a natural dam. Both sinking and uplifting seem to have taken place. Historian Myron Fuller wrote:

> The main movement along the lake appears to have been downward and was due in part to a general depression and in part to faulting. The uplift at the foot of the lake seems to have formed a part of the general uplift of the Tiptonville Dome. The line between the uplift and submerged lands at the south end of the lake is so sharp that it suggests faulting or at least a very sharp flexure.

Shaw's Park with John Steel Shaw and his family including twin boys, one of whom is Claude "Sharpie" Shaw dated 1904.

Photograph courtesy of Sharon Shaw Fowler Cunningham

Lillian Lyon Crossley
Photographed by Albert Gainer at Walnut Log - May 17-23, 1923.
She married Stephen Blackstone Crossley - first game warden at
Reelfoot Lake. The identity of the child is not known.

THE EARLY YEARS OF REELFOOT

In the early years of the lake, there were few inhabitants. The ground still trembled and shocks were felt for the next eleven years at irregular intervals. The Mississippi River was like a wild thing, flooding the lowlands and washing through Reelfoot each winter and spring. Early hunters in the area tell of a bounty of wildlife. People passing through the area didn't establish permanent homes because of the unsettled land and water. Most of the early residents settled along the Mississippi River bank or in the Obion County area. At this time there was no Tiptonville or Union City, both having been founded in the 1850's.

Famous hunter and politician David Crockett was one of the first settlers in this area. In his Autobiography, he tells of his coming to the Reelfoot region:

> Having returned from the legislature, I determined to make another move, and so I took my eldest son with me, and a young man by the name of Abram Henry, and cut out for the Obion. I selected a spot when I got there, where I determined to settle; and the nearest house to it was seven miles, the next nearest was fifteen, and so on to twenty. It was a complete wilderness, and full of Indians who were hunting. Game was plenty of every kind, which suited me exactly, as I was always fond of hunting...I made enough corn to do me, and during that spring, I killed ten bears, and a great abundance of deer. But in all this time, we saw the face of no white person except Mr. Owen's family and a few passengers, who went out there looking at the country...I gathered my corn and then set out for my Fall's hunt. This was in the last of October, 1822. I found bear very plentiful, and indeed, all sorts of game and wild varmints, except buffalo...I worked on with my hands till the bears got fat, and then I turned out to hunting to lay in a supply of meat.I soon

I soon killed and salted down as many as necessary for my family; but about this time one of my old neighbors, who had settled down on the lake, came to my house and told me he wanted me to go down and kill some bears about in his parts. He said they were extremely fat, and very plentiful. We hunted out the week, and in that time we killed seventeen, all of them first rate.

The first settlers around the lake were hunters, fishermen and trappers. The only settled area around the bank of the lake was the Wheeling community at the base of the bluffs. The people who lived around the lake lived in tent camps or in cabins built on stilts because of the spring floods.

The people were a hardy lot and very independent. They felt Reelfoot Lake and the land around it was their own private domain.

The settlement of Wheeling was founded in 1858, north of the present location of Samburg, where Highway 22 crosses Indian Creek. At one time all the permanent Reelfoot settlers lived here, close to the bluff. The settlement had several hundred residents, a hotel, stores, blacksmith shop, and a church. One of the stores was owned by Bernard Samberg, a German who settled there and owned most of the land in the Indian Creek area. The Samburg community is named after this merchant. He sold his store to John Shaw, owner of Shaw's Park, and moved from the area about 1895. It was about the same year that the community of Wheeling officially became known as Samburg. With a slightly different spelling from the merchant's name.

The area around the general store was known as Shaw's Park, and camping was allowed. There was a well and boat dock available for public use. After the levee system stopped flooding, most of the people left old Samburg and moved nearer the lake to Samburg's present location.

Stephen Blackstone Crossley
The husband of Lillian Lyon Crossley
and first game warden at Reelfoot Lake

An article from the Union City Commercial, July 1903, which had been through a fire at the Burdick Building was recently recovered and copied. The article is filled with information about the early years of Reelfoot Lake and follows in its entirety:

A THREE DAY'S TRIP AROUND REELFOOT LAKE

Its different points of importance-
Distance and Direction from each other

Fishing with a hook and line
where the waters ripple out;
"Bobbling" with a bob that's red-O it's fine
When the perch and trout are out.
Working up the sparkling shallows
Where the sun and water hallows;
Laughing, tumbling, falling in.
Fishing with a hook and line,
Ain't it fine!

The following condensed description of this celebrated fishing and hunting resort has been kindly furnished me by Mr. Pratt, "mine host" of that well kept hostelry, the Samburg Hotel. While this sketch is not supposed to be a complete pen picture of Reelfoot Lake, it is, nevertheless, concise and correct as to the principal points on the lake, their direction and distance from each other, and is the first and fullest thing of the kind ever published about the lake. It has been corrected and verified by Mr. J. C. Burdick and Mr. Bud Wade, and can be relied upon as correct and a safe guide to any part of the lake.

The extent of the fishing on this lake is a hard matter to determine. The regular fishermen, as a rule live here the year round, and are mostly married men with families, industrious and hard working, men who are good citizens, trying to rear and educate their children in a commendable manner, and who have made Reelfoot Lake quite a different place from what it was several years ago.

There are about five hundred and fifty men who make a living on the lake by fishing. There are different ways of fishing -- trot line, pole (bobbing for trout), pole fishing for perch, and trammel net fishing is the most in use now, besides the expensive seine run by Mr. Burdick's seine crew. About one thousand byke or set-nets are used from September 15th to April 15th. Many of the regular fishermen are farming at present and not fishing, but are getting their tackle ready for the fall and winter.

BURDICK'S DOCK AT SAMBURG

A few hundred yards north of Samburg is Mr. Burdick's principal dock, managed by Wash Reed, as thorough, attentive and business-like gentleman as you will meet anywhere. He receives the fish as they are brought in by the boats, washes them in ice water (dressing certain varieties), puts them in large ice boxes, ready to be packed in ice in the wagons which leave the dock every evening about 6 o'clock for Union City. Mr. Reed also furnishes each man, as his "catch" is weighed, with an itemized ticket of the different kinds of fish caught, the total value, etc., which ticket can be "cashed in" at any time and is commercial paper on the lake, as good as the cash or a bank check. To give a better idea of the number of men in the fishing industry, the following names of fishermen are given, whose boats come to this dock twice a day during this, the dull season, to dispose of their fish:

C. M. Downing, R. E. Wallace, J. W. Wilson, W. L. Glenn, Joe Johnson, Tom Yates, Tom Wilson, George Grooms, W. H. Webster, Lee Ford, Andy Pounds, Tom Owens, Matt Wallace, Will Hays, Frank Ferringer, Albert Dexter, Martin Leonard, Erv Agnew, J .W. Yarborough, Charlie Parkerson, W. E. Pratt, C. H. Carroll, Joe Yarbrough, Frank Daily, Henry Tarkington, Fayette Tarkington, Dave Quillen, Will Owens, George Sparks, Charles Allen, A. B. Allen, Allen Dowdy, John Bell, Jim Bell, Jeff Bell, R. L. Wallace, Dick Fish, Walter Cole, Bob Cole, John Cochran, George Hutchcraft, Charles Hutchcraft, Bob Matheny, Bob Reed, Herbert Anderson, S. B. Crosley, O. P. Downing, A. W. Reed, Dave Martin, Fred Burdick, John Davis and Bill Thomas.

SEINE CREW: J. H. Fox, Joe Brady, Fred Bramham, Sam Tate and hundreds of others who are now farming and will commence fishing in September.

Left to right: Wendall, Bud and Melvin Morris . . .
all commercial fishermen.

John Steel Shaw standing in Shaw's Park
which he owned. Note the white wash on
the trees which marked the high waterline.
Photograph courtesy of Sharon Shaw Fowler Cunningham

SHAW'S PARK

Starting from Samburg west, or a little south of west, the first point of interest is Shaw's Park, half a mile below Burdick's dock. Here Mr. Shaw has set aside a handsome place for the public, where people can camp with their families free of charge. The park contains eight acres and is a level, high, dry and beautiful woods lot picturesquely fringed on the lake side with tall, majestic cypress, and shaded throughout with hickory, ash, elm, and oak trees. It has just been mowed and cleared of all underbrush and furnished with a well of good cold water. A general grocery and dry goods store is just at the entrance to the park, and Shaw & Pleasant's dock is also located here, operated by that thorough fisherman and gentleman, Mr. Charley Downing.

GUM POINT

The next place of interest, one mile southwest down the shore of the lake, is Gum Point, a fishing camp, composed of C. M. Downing, J. W. Wilson and R. E. Wallace. This is one of the well-known places on the lake, and these men are all experienced fishermen, and have one of the largest tackles here -- the three combined fishing about 250 setnets. In speaking of J. W. Wilson, I expect I should say, "Finger Jim" as he is generally known by that patronymic. C. M. Downing is also in business in Hornbeak in a general store. R. E. Wallace is better known as "Little Bob" to distinguish him from R. L. Wallace, who by-the-way, is 6'4-1/2" in his stocking feet, and an A-1 fisherman. "Little Bob" is one of the hardest working men on the lake and catches many fish.

GUM POINT DRIFT

Directly opposite Gum Point, a quarter of a mile out in the lake, is Gum Point Drift, containing forty or fifty acres of green cypress trees, in water from three to eight feet deep and among these trees large logs have become immovable and lodged, among which has grown up brush, "bonnets" and rose bushes, thus forming a floating island or garden, where lovers and all well behaved and well-regulated pleasure parties from forty States, more or less, love to go "a-fishin", and where they catch many perch, trout, occasionally a "ducking" and sometimes an alligator (gar): Your fellow-townsman, Mr. Russ Garth, once caught all the above mentioned at this place.

WILLOWVILLE BOOM

Coming back to the shore of the lake from Gum Point Drift, we paddled on down to Willowville Boom, about two miles below Gum Point. Here is the camp of Martin Leonard and sons and several others.

LOG SLOUGH

Next down the shore is Log Slough, one mile south of Willowville Boom. Here is a camp which belongs to Ike Johnson.

BROAD SLOUGH

About one mile further on is Broad Slough, where there is another camp.

BLACK BAYOU

Black Bayou, three quarters of a mile from Broad Slough, comes next, with several camps.

CAMPBELL'S POINT

The next is Campbell's Point, one mile southwest, in Lake County. Here begins the great pecan forest, where pecans are almost as plentiful in the fall of the year as fish in the lake. Near here also is the celebrated "Washout", a sunken, weird, scary-looking place, a place which reminds one of an inferno (sic), and causing a sort of sinking, smothering feeling to look at it. It was at this place that Major Harris (deceased) proposed to drain the lake by connecting the two with a canal. George C. Campbell is postmaster here, the post office being called Blue Bank Bayou. This is one of the oldest places on the lake. Mr. Campbell is one of the oldest fishermen here, having been born and reared at this place. He is at present, and has been for many years, running a general store. He owns the place where he does business; is as pleasant and straightforward a man as one will see anywhere.

We have now passed the southernmost point of the lake, and are now turning west and north of the other side.

WHITE'S LANDING

Two miles northwest of Campbell's is White's Landing. Just why it is called White's Landing is an unknown problem, unless a Mr. White was the first civilized man who ever got ashore here through the mud, cypress trees, cutgrass, etc. However, when the lake is low and the shores dried out, one can land here without hip boots; and when once on terra firma, it is but a short two miles to the wonderfully growing and progressive town, Tiptonville, the capital of Lake County, on the Mississippi River.

KEYSTONE MILLSITE

Keystone Millsite is about three-fourths of a mile northwest of White's Landing, and one and a quarter miles farther north is the Old Distillery Place, now known as Champs Mill. Following around Champs Pocket about two miles, we come to:

GREEN POINT

This is a great fishing section also. Next in order, commencing at Green Point, is Swan Basin, a half-oval, bay-looking place, where formerly countless numbers of swans congregated to sing their "dying song" -- when the lucky hunter got close enough!

CANEY ISLAND

Caney Island is one mile southeast of Green Point and is one of the best trouting places on the lake. Mr. W. H. Webster and family are comfortably located on this island and he and his boys and boarders catch immense numbers of fish.

CHOCTAW ISLAND

Choctaw Island is a stone's throw southeast of Caney and is one of the prettiest islands in the lake. Choctaw Basin and:

GREEN ISLAND

Green Island, about three-fourths of a mile southeast, comes next with several fishing camps. Mr. Burdick makes this section headquarters for his immense seine, with which he catches great quantities of catfish, buffalo, spoonbill (mostly spoonbill) and other monsters of the "briney deep!"

This is one of the most beautiful spots on Reelfoot Lake as well as one of the best fishing grounds. Mr. Burdick has a camp here of several men, which he maintains winter and summer. The amount of fish that he catches here in the course of a year is enormous. W. E. Pratt also has a house on logs here in which he stays during the winter. He also runs a line of setnets and shoots ducks. Fred Burdick and Jim Bell are camping on this island and running a trammel net at present.

Paddling northeast one mile and a-half we come to:

RAT ISLAND

On this island is a good camping place. This is one of the best duck shooting places on the lake. What is called "The Meadows" is above this island, reached by going through Walnut Log. They are composed of small lakes and sloughs for miles.

Between Green and Rat Islands lies a part of Moultrie Field (Grassy Bend) in passing over which when the lake is low and clear, is like sailing over garden after garden of beautiful and vari-colored flowers (grasses, moss and ferns growing at the bottom of the lake at a depth of three to five feet), among which can be seen millions of perch -- red, white, blue, purple, black and brown, -- flashing and sporting beneath. It is well worth a trip to the lake to visit this enchanted spot alone, where "bonnets" three and four feet in circumference and golden and silver water lilies (especially in July and August) bedeck the surface of the crystal-clear water.

STARVED ISLAND*

Still traveling northeast up the lake and across Grassy Bend, Starved Island is the next camping ground. Here, there are three islands and camping grounds on each. This is the heart of the fishing country. Con Young and John Page have a house on one of these. They trap, fish and hunt. During the Civil War, refugees from the "conscript" would hide on the largest of these islands, and at times during the

45

winter, the ice between the island and the shore was too thick for the boats to get through it and too thin to be walked over, so that some of these refugees were confined there at the point of starvation. Hence the name "Starved Island."

HORSE ISLAND**

Horse Island, one mile east, and "Rag Point" three quarters of a mile southeast, are in this part of the lake. Cole Brothers here is another firm that fish a big tackle -- last season fishing 110 set nets. Horse Island gets its name from the fact that "once upon a time" a dead horse was found here, which could not be accounted for, and supposed (Jonah-like) to have been vomited up by one of the big leather-headed catfish that navigate this part of the lake.

BREWER BAR

This is two miles north. The old Nashville Club-house is at the head of this bar. The old landing was the property of Nashville men and was a great place for sport, but has been abandoned for some years. Henry Brady still lives close by and runs a big tackle; he also is an extensive farmer. Barney Brewer was born and reared here and has lived on this spot forty-five years, and is a successful fisher-man. Coming across this side again, three and a half miles from the Nashville Clubhouse, we come to P. C. Wards at:

WALNUT LOG LANDING

Ward's Dock is located here and run by P. C. Ward. He is in the fish and game business; also has a general store and hotel. Has rented the upper part of the lake from Mr. Burdick, and gets what fish are caught. He is also postmaster here and runs a really large new good hotel, where visitors and pleasure parties can rely on being hospitably cared for and at very reasonable rates. Long Point is about two miles northwest of Walnut Log and has several camping places.

About three miles north of Long Point is Ratcliffe Island, another old camping-place. From Walnut Log, paddling southwest two miles, the next place is:

GRASSY ISLAND POINT

Here are several camps and clubhouses. Coming southwest down the lake two miles you come to:

IDLEWILD

This is three miles and a half southwest of Spout Springs. Idlewild at one time was a pleasant hostelry, kept last by P. R. Nolen, deceased, but is now only occupied by a fisherman and his family. It is really a picturesque and beautiful spot. Thence south two miles and a half is:

WADE'S (BURDICK) DOCK

This place is sometimes called "Lake Center", being very near the center of the lake, and is one of the very best of landings. From here we paddle two miles west and south back to Mr. Burdick's other dock at Samburg, our starting point -- having fished, shouted, laughed, wondered and wandered all over Reelfoot Lake, and enjoyed ourselves for three of the shortest (happiest) days of a lifetime and paddled over forty-five miles. Are you tired? Yes, perhaps you are, and well prepared to enjoy a good supper and a sweet night's sleep. But are you satiated-sorry you went with us? If so, you are not a gentleman nor a scholar, nor a judge of a good time!

ISLANDS ON REELFOOT LAKE

Caney, Choctaw, Green, Rat, Little Rat, Nick's Towheads, Upper Starved, Lower Starved, Starved Island Towhead, Horse Island (from upper cut-off), Willow Towhead, Try Towhead, Excy Island, T. Island, Grassy Island, Brewer Bar Towheads (strip of land lying between the Big Slough and main lake commencing at the old canal just above the old Carpenter Hotel, running down the lake to where the Big Slough comes out into the main lake), Long Point (from Kentucky line down to the point), Ratcliffe Island, Green Point, near Swan Basin.

Places not specially mentioned; commencing at Kentucky State Line: Otter Pond, Beaver Dam, Hackle Slough, Joe Arm, Owen Slough, Goose Pond Slough, Bayou de Chein, Glory Hole, Eastrich Arm, Rittenhouse Basin, Roney Basin, Nick's Basin, Cary Basin, Longview, Carey Towheads, Snaggy Slough, Try Timber, Try Opening, Lone Cypress, Long Pond, Buzzard Slough, Buzzard Basin, Buzzard Timber, Burnt Woods, Big Sandy, Shallow Place, Round Cypress, Buck Basin, Willow Point, Kate's Cracklin Gourd, Starved Ponds, Forked Pond (several listed, illegible), Walnut Gap, Eagle Nest Timber, Round Drift, Nick's Field, Lee Basin, Snider Basin, Moultrie Field, Bell Timber, Corn Landing, Ferry Point, Box Slough, Lower Ferry Point, Catfish Channel, Half Moon Basin, Lower Blue Basin, Choctaw Basin, Swan Gap, Swan Basin, Lamb Bar, Sunk Poplar Float Road, Big Slough and Champs Pocket.

REELFOOT ISLANDS LEASED

"Judge Harris has leased to J. C. Burdick, who now owns the hunting and fishing privileges for profit, all the islands of the lake, some thirty-five or forty in number. Mr. Burdick will use the islands at present for camping grounds for his fishermen, and for all others who wish to fish and hunt for pleasure. As soon as the Tiptonville levee is completed, making the islands tillable, they will be converted into some of the productive farms in Tennessee." -- from Nashville American, July 18.

Since the litigation over the ownership of Reelfoot Lake commenced several years ago, many of the older fishermen have become somewhat uncertain and discouraged, and some quit fishing. However, many are rallying again, and recognize the fact that "there are as good fish in the sea as have ever been caught" and are preparing for the extensive fishing this fall. Last season Mr. Burdick furnished $4,000.00 worth of tackle, and will this season have furnished $7,000.00 worth. This tackle is turned over to the fishermen to be paid for out of the profits of their fishing and become their property. The new seine just sent to the lake (Mr. Burdick's ' private property) cost $600.00 and weighs 2,750 pounds.

In concluding this brief description of Reelfoot Lake, I would say that there are many places not especially mentioned, such as Spain's Point, Grassy Bend, Race Course, Forked Pond, Chapa Pocket, Kate's Gourd, Bayou de Chein, Reelfoot and Indian Creeks, etc., and to give the names of all the fishermen would be a job I would not undertake. But there is one thing sure, in any camp here, if you should step in, you would be received in a courteous manner and asked to make yourself at home. Nowhere will you find a warmer greeting or greater hospitality.

-LONE FISHERMAN

*Starved Island has, over the years, become Starve Island-and is so called elsewhere in this book.
**Local historian, Ed Hogg, states that Horse Island got its name because that is where the locals hid their horses from the Union soldiers during the Civil War-Author.

*This picture was taken from a
post card in Trenton, TN and has
been photo enhanced by Robert E. Clendenin, Jr.*

THE NIGHT RIDER ERA
AND STATE OWNERSHIP

In the early 1900's Tiptonville businessman J. C. Harris acquired title to most all the lands under and around Reelfoot Lake. His intentions were to drain the lake, but after several court battles with riparian owners, he was restrained by injunction.

In 1902 the West Tennessee Land Company was formed to obtain the holdings of J. C. Harris, the interests of the small landowners, and the area under the lake. The people around the lake felt betrayed by their lawyers, who had joined forces to form the land company and control fishing rights on the lake.

When the land company acquired the tracts of land around the lake not covered by the original grants, they claimed and assumed exclusive control within the boundary of the property. The professional fishermen of the lake were compelled to sell their fish only to the Reelfoot Game and Fish Company wholesale and retail dealers, who paid a royalty of one-half cent a pound to the West Tennessee Land Company for the exclusive right. Much dissatisfaction arose among the fishermen, for they thought that the dealers and the land company were being enriched at their expense, since there was no longer any competition for their catch, and the price of fish was low. Some of them tried to compete in distribution with the lessees just mentioned, but they were enjoined by the courts from all fishing for profit on the lake.

The people of the lake region, accustomed to unrestricted hunting and fishing on the lake, bitterly resented the efforts of the West Tennessee Land Company to deprive them of these privileges upon the claim of title and ownership and right to control as private property. This resentment led to the "Night Rider" activities of 1908.

The "Night Riders" was a secret, oath-bound organization operating in Tennessee and Kentucky attempting to force tobacco raisers to join an association for price control of their crop. To resist the West Tennessee Land Company's ownership of the lake, a branch of "Night Riders" was formed in the Reelfoot region, numbering, finally, an estimated 200 members.

The early activities of the Reelfoot "Night Riders" consisted of sending anonymous threatening letters to those connected with the West Tennessee Land Company and Reelfoot Fish and Game Company. Several houses, a small storehouse and the fish dock operated by Reelfoot Fish and Game were burned. Due to the amount of public sympathy generated in the belief that the fishermen and farmers had been greatly wronged under the cloak of the law, no one was punished for these crimes.

As the summer of 1908 advanced, the number of "Night Riders" increased, and the group's activities became more vigilante in nature, not limited to the original cause, but levied against anyone who had incurred the wrath of gang members: people were whipped, offices ransacked, private property destroyed.

In October 1908, two stockholders in the West Tennessee Land Company, Captain Quentin Rankin and Colonel R. Z. Taylor, were in the Reelfoot area inspecting the 3,600 acre strip of land known as Grassy Island for leasing. They were hoteled in Walnut Log, on the banks of Bayou de Chien (which empties into Reelfoot Lake) and had retired for the night.

They were awakened by a knock on the door, which when opened, revealed a number of masked men. The men ordered Rankin and Taylor to dress and accompany them. On a bluff east of town, the group halted. There began an interrogation of Colonel Taylor with regard to the legalities of the Reelfoot acquisition. He was struck and put under guard while a number of the group moved ten to fifteen feet away toward the edge of the lake, taking Captain Rankin with them.

At a leaning ash tree, forked eight or ten feet above the ground, they stopped and placed a rope around Rankin's neck. While being pulled from the ground, Rankin protested that they were killing him; he was told that was what the men intended to do.

Immediately a shot was fired, and then more shots, ending Rankin's life. Colonel Taylor, foreseeing his own fate, chose this time of distraction to jump into the bayou-attempting escape. Although many shots were fired at the fleeing figure and the "Night Riders" assumed him dead, Taylor survived. He traveled westward for about two days to the home of a friend where he was cared for.

Meanwhile, the moral conscience of the nation (and the State) was shocked upon learning of the tragedy. Search parties were sent to recover Taylor's body, presuming his death along with Rankin. The Governor of Tennessee offered a reward for arrest and conviction of the band and dispatched state troops to capture the "Night Riders."

More than fifty prisoners were taken and arraigned before a special grand jury. Several confessions were made regarding the activities of the gang and the murder. Some claimed membership under duress. Indictments of murder in the first degree were returned against eight members, who pleaded "not guilty" and went to trial in December 1908. The men were convicted of murder and sentenced to be executed by hanging. The case was reversed by the Supreme Court in April 1909, and removed for a new trial on technical grounds. Thereafter the prosecution appeared to languish, and there was no punishment meted out to those formerly convicted of murder.

The people, sure that their natural rights had been invaded by the private ownership of the lake, generated public sympathy that Reelfoot Lake, with its hunting and fishing rights, should not be subject to private ownership and control. The legislature of Tennessee in 1909, responded to this general view by passing an act in which the state claimed title to Reelfoot Lake and declared void the grants theretofore issued and laid on the soil under the waters.

Another act, passed by the same legislature, created a state game and fish preserve at Reelfoot Lake and in its preamble stated that this property should be held and controlled by the state for the use of all the people of the state. The legislature, in another act of the same session, made provision for the supervision and control of the property and the hunting and fishing rights as a state game and fish preserve for the use, benefit, and pleasure of all the citizens of the state.

The State of Tennessee became conscious of the need of adequate conservation laws. In 1915, the legislature passed an act for the creation of a Department of Game and Fish and provided for its maintenance. At one time, barrels of ducks and geese were shipped to the finest restaurants in the north on a weekly basis. In 1918, the Federal government stopped the sale of waterfowl and this ended the market hunting era of Reelfoot Lake.

Photography by Vern Sabin in 1922 and 1923

Dale Calhoun building my
new Reelfoot Lake boat in 1987.
I still use it today.

BOATS BY CALHOUN

The history of Reelfoot would not be complete without telling the Calhoun Reelfoot Lake Boat story. Arthur "Boone" Calhoun settled on Reelfoot in the mid-1800's and built his first Reelfoot boat with which to hunt and fish. His design was so popular he soon had a sideline that was to make his family famous. Three generations of Calhouns have been building boats on the lake; Boone, William and Dale, who is now 71 years of age. Few changes have been made in the original design, and the 118 year old pattern still hangs on Dale's shop wall for special boats.

In 1880 Fred Allen of Mammouth, Illinois came to hunt on Reelfoot Lake and promptly designed and patented the famous bow facing oars. The oars were the only method of propelling in the early days. Fred Allen was one of the first duck call makers, advertising his calls as early as 1882, and is considered a fore-runner to Glodo.

The Calhoun boat has been enlarged from the original twelve foot size to a giant eighteen and one-half feet. Motors, first used in the 1940's, were originally of the washing machine type. "The boats have been built out of cypress, mahogany, yellow poplar, and sassafras," Dale Calhoun said. But regardless of the lumber chosen, the design is the same. The flat-bottom boat is designed to slide over the Reelfoot stumps and is sought by sportsmen nationwide.

The bottom is made of seven-eights inch lumber, and the sides are cut from three-eights inch planks which are steamed in the vat used by his grandfather. The steaming process makes the wood supple so that it can be bent into shape and nailed. The boards are coated with "Wood Life"

and two layers of fiberglass, being finished with two coats of paint of the customer's choice. Calhoun says, if properly cared for, his boats will last a lifetime, and the best way to care for a Reelfoot boat is to keep it in the water.

Dale Calhoun purchased the patent and manufacturing rights to the Allen oar locks in 1959. He also hand makes the boat seats and oars for the locks, making the finished product completely customized. It takes about a week to build a Calhoun boat and put into it all the pride Dale has in doing it right.

Dale is likely to be the last of the Calhoun boat builders, and for that reason he constructed for me my last lake boat. It is eighteen feet long with a 32" bottom and a five inch rake in the bow to help it climb the high slosh. He has installed a twelve-horse engine in it, and a set of those fine Allen oars.

It's been eighteen years since he finished my boat. I enjoyed a visit with him last week. He is still doing what he likes to do best, building those great Reelfoot Lake boats.

He has added to the line a small boat that can be used as a coffee table with a set of stands. He is also building book shelves in lake boats standing on end for books and collectibles. My eighteen foot Calhoun boat is still in the water in the boathouse. It gives me much joy to use it on the lake. Life is good!

Photograph courtesy of Howard Harlan

THE BICYCLE SPOKE REELS

According to a 1940 "Ripley's Believe It or Not" article, the first bait-casting reel used by fishermen was an invention of some pre-1900 Reelfoot Lake fishermen. At one time, the reels were as well known and unique as the famous Reelfoot boats. According to Ed Hogg, no one knows who built the first one, but Charlie Allen, J. E. "Sundown" Cochran, Uncle Joe Spicer and Frank Dietzel all built them.

The reels were all built from bicycle spokes soldered together, and had a chrome hub that required a thumb brake; some had a leather patch to apply friction and control the speed of the reel.

The people on the lake used them faithfully on strong stiff rods and adhered to the philosophy of pulling and horsing the fish into the boat as quickly as possible to avoid all the underwater structures in the lake. The guides liked to tell their sports, "You can play with the fish all you want to after you get him IN the boat!"

It's been seventeen years since I researched the old Bicycle Spoke Reels Reelfoot Lake became famous for. At that time we only knew of six or seven made by three different Reelfoot families and one family in Union City, Tennessee. At the time of that writing, I didn't have one in my collection and I didn't have great hopes of aquiring one, but every now and then you get lucky. In 1995, I located the best made one I have ever seen and found a new maker, "Slingshot" Charlie Taylor.

The reel at the bottom was made by Frank Dietzel.
The rod and reel in the middle was made by Joe Spicer.
The reel at the top was made by J. E. "Sundown" Cochran.

Charlie Taylor's bicycle spoke reel
and homemade square steel rod with wooden handle.

REELFOOT LAKE DUCK CAMPS AND CLUBHOUSES

Reelfoot Lake was a famous hunting and fishing spot in the early eighteen and nineteen hundreds and groups of men formed sporting clubs to take advantage of the great hunting and fishing. The following is a history of the clubs from the 1880's until present day.

At least four of the clubs are still active today, enjoying the heritage and friendships their founding fathers started long ago.

UNION CITY OUTING CLUB

Most old timers in the Reelfoot Lake area will remember the Union City Outing Club. This club was formed in 1882 with ten members: Ed McAlister, George Danke, Herman Dietzel, John Semones, J. T. Williams, W. T. Latimer, Sid Herring, Charlie Keiser, Bill Nailing and Nully Pleasant.

They kept their boats at Taylor Point in Kirby Pocket where the state dock is now. They first used a tent camp close to the old hotel on the island where Victor Glodo, Sundown Cochran and Jack Hogg hunted, fished and guided.

Later, they moved to Grassy Island and in 1890 built the cabin pictured. Note that the name of the lodge was shown as the Union City Outing Club.

The cabin was a two-room affair with a huge bed in the front room. The bed was a huge frame with fence wire fastened across it, on which each man laid his own mattress, and they all slept together. The group was enlarged to include: Pink Bennett, Walker Tanner, Jack Hubbs, Fred Nailing, and Red Lanzer.

These men enjoyed the good hunting of this area. The average kill per person for opening week was 200 birds per day. These members were the first group of sportsmen to work for conservation on the lake. Their hunting was before the use of blinds in the area and they hunted Snaggy, Burnt Woods, Buzzard Slough and the Glory Hole before the refuges were established.

The lodge was moved in the early 1940's to Acorn Point where it was used by the club until it was sold to a club member, Red Armstrong, who replaced it with a nice home in 1972.

UNION CITY OUTING CLUB
(Written by the late Walton Crenshaw about 1968)

In 1883, a group of men went on an encampment at Reelfoot Lake. They camped on Horse Island. The group was made up of Ed McAlister, Jeff Williams, Nully Pleasant, Charlie Herring, John Semones, Herman Dietzel, John Mitchell, Clifford Joyner, Sr. and Joseph Roberts. There are many stories concerning this trip, including the many ducks killed and the size of the bass Ed McAlister caught; many tales enlarged with each telling.

They got up at two o'clock in the morning and hitched up the team. They loaded the wagon and met at Nailling-Keiser Hardware Co. on First St. in Union City. Then they started to Reelfoot Lake.

You can imagine what a problem it was to get everything they would need loaded in the wagon as they could not run up to Samburg every time they ran out of something they needed. Provisions had to be carried, bed clothes, tents, cooking utensils, etc., not to mention "snake bite medicine." From all indications, this was a most enjoyable trip and it was decided this would be an annual affair.

In 1887, the camping place was changed from Horse Island to Grassy Island, due most likely because it would be closer to the best hunting and fishing grounds. They camped in tents again and it was the same long trip with all the preparations to be made as in the other camp, but on this trip everything had to be hauled four miles farther out in the lake.

This was continued each year until 1892, when the club purchased a house from Charlie Allen with the stipulation that he could live in it except when the club came down for their annual hunt. It is certain that some members had dropped out of the club and some had been added.

In 1909, the club re-organized and built a new club-house on Grassy Island. This necessitated some expenditure and it was decided to take in some new members to help pay for the house. New members were: Bill Nailling, Charlie Keiser, Jake Gibbs, Charlie Burchard, John Joyner, and Dr. Butler; Charlie Herring and Herman Dietzel remained as old members. Some of the members went down and boxed in the sides and put in windows before the club went down for their camp.

The roof was donated by Nailling-Keiser Hardware Co. and was put on the first day the club came to camp. At that time, they did not have a kitchen or dining room and they used the old house of Charlie Allen for cooking and eating.

In 1911, a kitchen and dining room were added onto the new house. This was the home of the Union City Outing Club for the next thirty-one years.

During this time, new members were added as follows: H. Dietzel, H. and Lexie Williams, J. C. McRee, Alwayn Brevard, C. W. Carr, Cato Davis, Pink Bennett, W. E. Hudgins, Walker Tanner, Jack Hubbs, Sr., Wallace Latimer, Walton Crenshaw, Reece Alexander, Fred A. Nailling, E. C. Crenshaw, Phebus McAlister, Jack Hubbs, Jr., R. C. Joyner, Jr., W. Paul Nailling, John Caldwell, M. T. Warren, and Ben Herring.

After thirty-one years of living on Grassy Island in the new clubhouse, the island was taken over in 1942 by the State of Tennessee and the U. S. Fish and Wildlife Service and made a game reserve, forcing us to move. The state paid us $250 for our squatter's rights.

No camp was held in 1942 at the clubhouse, however Phebus McAlister, Jack Hubbs, Clifford Joyner, Jr., Ed Crenshaw, Fred Nailling, John Caldwell, and M. T. Warren rented a cabin from Charlie Henson near Box Slough and hunted from there.

During 1942, the old clubhouse was torn down by Sam Parkman, put on skiffs, and moved to Gum Point while waiting for a place to re-locate. We attempted to buy Booker's camp site on Rat Island. Negotiations were going forward and we thought the deal would be closed. So, we built about 300 feet of walkway from the saw grass into Booker's camp getting ready for transporting and building the clubhouse there. Four skiff loads of lumber were transported over there before the Booker heirs decided not to sell the land to us.

Then, we had to re-load the lumber and move back to Gum Point. During this same year, we purchased 100-foot frontage, at that time only a forest, on the lake from Ralph Hornbeak. Ralph told Mr. John Joyner that 100 feet from a certain oak tree either north or south would be alright for us to build the clubhouse on.

Arrangements were made with Sam Parkman to build the clubhouse for $150. He built the clubhouse using the same lumber that had been transported from Grassy Island, with a few refinements added, with an extra expenditure of $10, which was an engineering marvel, as Mr. Parkman had marked where each piece of lumber came from in the old house and put it back in the same place as before. After the house was built, Ralph Hornbeak told us we had built 100 feet from the wrong oak tree, so we had to move it about 100 feet south of its location to the place where it is now.

New members were added: Bill Keiser, A. T. Cloar, R. C. Reynolds, Jack Burdick, H. A. Lanzer, and R. H. Armstrong. In 1961, Bill Latimer was added, and in 1966 Jack Bratton.

This was the oldest clubhouse that has continued operations without a break for eighty years. On November 21, 1967, the club was disbanded and sold to a member, Red Armstrong.

I am so glad Walton Crenshaw wrote the history of this club. The effort put forth to camp at Reelfoot Lake in early times is so fascinating. Also, this club paid taxes each year on the Union City acre that the state finally took over.

Top Picture: Joe Foxall and Larry Hickerson
Bottom Picture: George Thomas, Club President and Senior Member,
is still regularly enjoying the club.

DIXIE ROD AND GUN CLUB

This club was organized in 1922, by the following group of Union City, Tennessee hunters: W. H. Harris, T. R. Reynolds, O. H. Danke, William McAdoo, O. H. Cobb, Clarence Guill, John Wadell, R. C. Jackson, C. E. Beck, Reagor Motlow, Louis McAdoo, W. O. Kelly, Robert Pardue, Spencer Millard, O. L. Dalton, Ed Marshall, Curtis Verhine, J. W. Jones, Ed Parks, Paul Johnson, Claude Botts, A. C. Houser, Thurman Talley, Hugh Smith, A. Hamilton and honorary member Lem Motlow. The purpose of the club "shall be recreation and pleasure obtained from hunting and fishing and not for profit."

Photo by Vern Sabin

70

Blue Wing Clubhouse built on Grassy Island after 1912.
Photograph by Henry Lupton

Current clubhouse built around 1946. Picture taken in 1951.
The fallen hunter is the author as a youth.

BLUE WING CLUB

This club was organized in 1885 with fourteen founders from Clarksville, Tennessee and Mayfield, Kentucky. The founding members were: C. T. Young, E. C. Bates, Louis G. Wood, J .C. Kendrick, T. L. Porter, Len Blanton, Bill Kleeman, Frank Beaumont, John West, H. E. Dibble, Ed Pierce, T. L. Ledbetter and J. E. Elder.

In 1889, the club received a state charter with additional members and J. C. Harris was an honorary member from Tiptonville. In the early days it took seventeen hours to reach Reelfoot from Clarksville riding the train first to McKenzie; changing trains and on to Hickman, Kentucky. From Hickman they went by horse and wagon arriving at Walnut Log where they boarded flat bottomed skiffs for the trip to the club house. Most hunting and fishing trips were for a week or more and they took a black couple with them to cook and clean.

The Blue Wing sold their property on Grassey Island to the State of Tennessee in 1930 leasing back for several years until property could be purchased on the northwest side of the lake. The present club location is a two acre site purchased in the mid 1940's and the two story block house was built about 1946.

In 1938 the membership was limited to twenty five for a fee of two hundred fifty dollars. The sons of many of this membership are still active today enjoying great fishing and fellowship.

Billy Patch (1896 - 1987) Blue Wing Club
He was the mentor and patriarch from Clarksville.
He was one of the first men I guided as a teenager. His son and
son-in-law are still active in the club. Note the live decoy on the front
of the boat and the coop on the back. Guide is Paul Strader.

Black Jack Club members enjoy great fellowship and sportsman opportunities.

BLACK JACK HUNTING CLUB

This club was organized in 1923 with a Clarksville membership of twelve. Fees were one hundred fifty dollars and dues were five dollars per year. Members carried their own servants and furnished their food for each encampment. Members were not allowed to take shells with shot larger than #1 on the lake. If they did, they were fined not less than one dollar nor more than five dollars. Hubert Woods was head guide and caretaker. He lived close by with his family in a house on stilts.

The cooks wore white jackets, and the head cook a white chef's hat. After supper the members drank straight whiskey while sitting around listening to an old battery radio. They followed the whiskey with licks on a King Leo candy stick.

This club is still active and they have great fellowship; my duck call collecting buddy, Bill Organ, is a member and I enjoyed a fellowship with them in 2004.

In the beginning, they came by car to the lake on a lot of gravel roads and crossed the lake from Walnut Log by boat to the clubhouse.

Donna rowing in the moonlight.

FULTON RED WING CLUB

I don't know the start up date for this club but it was located at lake center above the Dixie Rod and Gun Club. The picture shows a great hunting day in the early 1930's. Some of the men in the picture were Leslie H. Weaks, Clyde Williams and Dr. J. C. Scruggs. This club was still active until some time in the 1950's.

Shady Rest built in 1946.

The cabin had been painted red in 1978.
Look at my custom built Ford Bronco. It would go anywhere!

CALDWELL'S SHADY REST

My dad, Chester, built his dream cabin in 1946 after the close of World War II. He bought a two acre tract from a Mrs. Isbell and used local labor to construct the concrete block building. It had two large rooms, front and back, a bathroom with no hot water heater and an unfinished loft for storage. It took almost a year before we had the tin roof on. The septic tank in a hand dug hole took forever. We also had to clear the lot and build a dock. The whole family worked on it on the weekends.

Time spent here was a great time for our family. We fished, hunted, hiked, picnicked and entertained a wide variety of family and friends. Dad and I built our blind across the lake on the Mud Basin and Buzzard Slough duck crossing and enjoyed steady shooting there till the late 1960's.

In 1955 and 1956, Dad fulfilled a dream to own a small motel on the lake for his retirement and it was completed in early 1956. When I was in college at University of Tennessee at Martin, I helped him during weekends, holidays, and between quarters by working on the dock and guiding hunters and fishermen from the area. Learning to work with people was great training for my future business. Dad sold the little motel in the early 1960's to a Tiptonville football coach and it is now owned by Bill and Candy Curlin and renamed The Sportsman. The old duck blind is owned by my friend Barry Duncan of Union City, TN and still has good hunting and fellowship. It's one of the oldest blinds on the lake.

Walnut Log Lodge floated on cypress logs. Burned in 1919.
This hotel was built by P. C. Ward - land was purchased from J. C. Burdick, Sr. in 1900.
Photograph courtesy of Sharon Shaw Fowler Cunningham

Hunt Roper, Charles Keiser and Jim Major Cabin
Photograph courtesy of Jim Major

Cleeman Club at Gray's Camp was torn down in the early 1970's.
Photograph courtesy of Onis Strader

Old Samburg Hotel. Note the wooden decoys and ducks in foreground.
Photograph courtesy of Sharon Shaw Fowler Cunningham

Photograph by Louis Mikel (Reelfoot guide)

Tornado at Reelfoot Lake in May of 2000.

Reelfoot Lake sunset by Donna Caldwell.

Photographs by Robert E. Clendenin, Jr.

REELFOOT LAKE 2005

Reelfoot Lake today is still, I think, the most beautiful place on earth. I never spend a moment on the waters that I don't thank God for this special place. I live here now and the last thirteen years have been some of the greatest times of my life. I am going to share with you most of the changes on the lake and update on the activities that people enjoy.

I think the overall lake is in better shape now than it's been in years. The water quality is better and the silt coming into the lake has been minimized. We now have a silt pump and an aqua track hoe to clean out the ditches, sloughs and duck holes. This equipment is much better than the old cookie cutter used years ago which was broken most of the time.

The old spillway is still being used, but repairs have been made to it and outside of a small leak, it's still doing the job it was built for in the 1930's. The land has been purchased for the routing of the new spillway and the state of Tennessee has undertaken it as their project, so in the next few years we could have a new one.

A couple of years ago the state stopped the netting of game fish in Reelfoot and this has made giant steps to improve the quality of fishing in the lake. It's not unusual to have over five hundred boats on the water on a pretty spring day. The crappie, bass and bluegill are all larger on the average than they were five years ago.

Several of the access areas to the lake have been improved so there is more opportunity to bring your own boat to use while hunting and fishing on the lake. This has increased use of the lake by local sportsmen, along with the quality of the sport available.

During the winter a popular thing is eagle watching. Many people make an annual pilgrimage to observe these great birds. The numbers visible on the lake are down to around fifty and most of these are year around residents of the lake. It is thought that since the cessation of the netting of game fish (with the throwing out of unwanted fish) and the drop in number of ducks and geese migrating through, there is no longer as much easy food on the lake for the winter migrating eagles to find, and they are now wintering on catfish ponds in surrounding areas. The presence of five or six active nests in the area may turn eagle watching into a year around activity.

The fall consists of two great local activities. One of these is the Arts and Crafts Festival and is the best craft fair of its type in this part of the country. It takes place the first weekend in October, one of the prettiest times of year at Reelfoot. Over twenty thousand people come each year to see unique things and shop for early Christmas presents. The other event is the Reelfoot Waterfowl Festival, started in 1990 by Son Cochran, John Asbille and me. Several hundred people come each year to participate in the Duck Calling Contest, visit their hunting buddies and see all the new duck stuff. This event has rotated each year in the early fall months and is now run by Son and Bonnie's daughter and son, Helen Jean Pierce and Johnny Cochran.

One of the favorite past times of the local residents of the lake is the duck and goose hunting season. This season has really changed. The geese no longer come this far south and now if you harvest one, it is a trophy much like the wild turkey. We are in our sixth year of our six duck limit with sixty days to hunt. The great years of the late nineties are gone and the refuges are growing up; the duck and wildlife food is being eaten by Snow Geese. The last four years have been much slower for the duck and goose hunter. I expect the limit and season will be cut in the future to give the birds the opportunity to come back. We need a shorter season and four birds. A great addition to the hunting opportunity has been the handicap area on the west side of the lake. It benefits disadvantaged hunters from the surrounding area each year. It was a project of my son, Harold, and the family is still interested in it.

Waterfowl Festival
Micah Caldwell, Donna Caldwell, Bonnie Cochran, Rob Caldwell and Johnny Cochran

Harold Caldwell and John Leslie at the handicap area.

Photograph by Jim Johnson

Photograph from 1980 of southern part of Reelfoot Lake.

Photography courtesy of Baughn Merideth

Reelfoot Ranger Oil Company oil well. Dug to a
total depth of 1,240 feet. A dry well, abandoned, as
were all six drilled in Reelfoot Lake area between 1915 and
1939. My dad said a lot of Obion County businessmen lost money
on the venture. Note the area is the location of the Night Rider hang-
ing in 1909 at the Walnut Log Hotel pictured on right side of the picture.
Photograph by Vern Sabin

Photograph courtesy of Jim Johnson

Photograph by Robert E. Clendenin, Jr.

REELFOOT LAKE DUCK CALLS

THE MAGNIFICENT SEVEN
DUCK CALL MAKERS OF REELFOOT LAKE

Some of the call collectors attempt to collect every type of call; others focus on the best calls. This section of the book is not about all the Reelfoot call makers but the seven old-timers who made the best calls and had the most impact on the duck call making craft. I am giving information about each call maker in detail with lots of new photographs never seen before.

Duck call collecting has grown in popularity in the last eighteen years since our association was formed. We now have almost five hundred members, a quarterly newsletter, a membership book and the dues are still only $25.00 per year. If you are interested in joining Call Makers and Collectors Assoc. of America please contact:

William Bailey
137 Kingswood Drive
Clarksville, TN 37043

One of the most exciting things I have been involved in has been my duck call collection and helping build call collecting interest. Every duck hunter is a potential duck call collector. Most of us have a box full of calls in our closet or gun room and this accumulation is the start of a collection. There are still a lot of good calls out there and you can never tell where your next treasure will turn up. When you collect old things, you live in two different times.

VICTOR GLODO, JR.
INVENTOR OF THE REELFOOT LAKE STYLE DUCK CALL

*Victor Glodo, Jr. Justice of the Peace
and market gunner at Fountain Bluff, IL.*

Victor Glodo, Jr.
Father of the American Duck Call

Victor was born in Illinois on June 18, 1845. In the course of his life he would become the most famous duck call maker of all time. His legacy would span over one hundred twenty five years in the area where his duck call invention is still being made in his home territory, Reelfoot Lake, with the same structure and form he used in the late 1860's.

Victor, Sr. was born in France in 1826 and came to the United States as a young man. Working as a farmer and carpenter, he settled near St. Louis, Illinois in the 1840's. There he met and married an Illinois woman, starting his family of two sons, Victor, Jr. in 1845 and John Nickolas in 1847. In the late 1850's the family moved to the Degognia Township in Jackson County. Victor Sr.

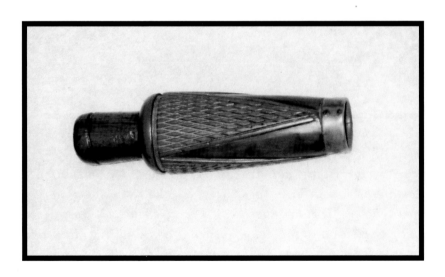

The Morris Glodo
The best example of his early call making. Note the copper brad fitted on the end of the call correcting a crack.

and Jr. joined the Union Army in 1862 and fought in the Civil War. Victor Sr. came home early after suffering heat stroke, but Victor, Jr. stayed on longer. Walter Albert Glodo was born to Victor Sr. and his second wife, Eliza E. Painter, in 1869.

After the Civil War, in 1865, shooting ducks for the market became a part of the Glodo's profession. During these years they invented the duck call known today as the Reelfoot Lake style. Because of the curved reed and wedge block with the flat tone board, I believe they were the original inventor, in other words, they didn't go by someone else's call type. Could he have made calls earlier? Sure, but many times need brings on invention and until market hunting became a way of life there was little need.

This Victor Glodo call traces back to Jake Gibbs (of the Remington Arms Co.). Tom Curry, a well known sportsman of the Glodo era from Brownsville, TN received the call from Gibbs and passed it on to the John Cochran family. The call is held together by a lead band on the stopper and barrel. It has raised checkering and rounded stopper that has often been copied. The barrel is of walnut, the stopper of heartwood birch. Unmistakably Glodo, it is one of the best examples of his work.
(From Howard Harlan Collection)

Between 1875 and 1880 the family moved to the Fountain Bluff area on the edge of the Big Lake Marsh where waterfowl hunting was some of the best in the county. A railroad and the Mississippi River were close making timely game shipments to the St. Louis area possible. In 1888 the Big Lake Marsh was drained and this possibly contributed to Victor Glodo, Jr. leaving the area. All of the Glodo brothers were making duck calls during this time frame. The Glodos were the first known call makers to checker their calls. John Nickolas and Albert's calls had flat top barrels and their inserts were tapered toward the front. Victor's duck calls had rounded shoulders and his quality was better than his brothers. His checkering, even though done with a home-made hand tool, was excellent quality, especially in the early years. All calls were hand made and show no lathe work. Even though they appear round, they are not.

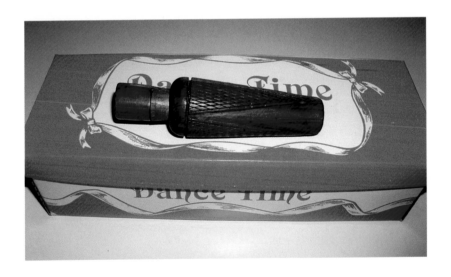

"Pink Shoe Box" Glodo duck call.
This call was found after a 10-year search. Two
Johnny Marsh duck calls were traded for it in 1990.

Last winter I paid a visit to the Fountain Bluff area and walked and drove over the area with Gene Korando, an Illinois duck call maker whose family has owned and farmed a lot of the Big Lake Marsh since it was drained. Parts of the hunting area can be seen today in depressions and sloughs that still mark the land. You can close your eyes and imagine the huge flights of ducks in the old days and hear a Glodo brother say, "Get on that bunch; they will work!"

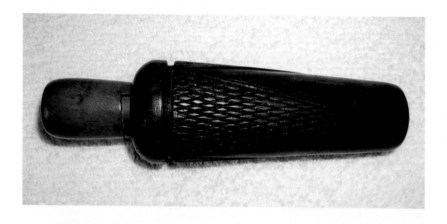

Another "early" Glodo call which shows his very fine work.

One of the last Victor Glodo duck calls made.
It was done for Roy Parkerson, Nath Parkerson's dad.

Victor Glodo, Jr. standing on the porch of
John Steel Shaw's store at Old Samburg at Reelfoot Lake in 1905.

The Reelfoot Lake Years

In 1891, Victor Glodo, Jr. moved south to the Reelfoot lake area. It was here that his legend and legacy became larger than life. Two locally famous writers, Nash Buckingham and Tom Turpin wrote about Victor Glodo in early twentieth century stories they wrote about duck calls. The first of these was written in 1928 by Nash Buckingham and the Glodo part of the story follows:

> Swamp angels and market hunters of that day, however mothered by apparent necessity were using hand made calls not much different from today's models. As in most contrivances, our best calls spring from those very early models. The most noted of early calls was the "Glodo"; made, I think, by a Frenchman famed for his prowess with gun and call on a once well-known southern Illinois marsh. My friend, Guy Ward, of Reelfoot Lake and trap shooting fame, is the proud possessor of an original Glodo. I have heard that as a reed producer and toner, Glodo's experimental turn for metal manipulation was little short of marvelous.

Tom Turpin wrote in 1931 in <u>Field and Stream</u> the following:

> After getting the opinion of many of the most expert duck callers in the country, I decided that the best model is the call produced by Glodo, an old-timer of the jack-knife-school of artists, who made his calls at Reelfoot Lake some twenty years ago. Glodo's model is on the same principle as the Beckhart and Hafer (*Slifer*), both of which are good calls and should satisfy any hunter. I prefer the Glodo for certain features; I think the groove is better shaped, the general proportions better and the reed wider and shorter.

Both of these men were duck call authorities in their time and have added to information we have about Glodo.

The following are excerpts from interviews with people who knew Glodo and lived in the area he did during his life at Reelfoot.

In the late 1980's I interviewed Mrs. Effe Hogg whose husband lived in a camp on Starve Island close to the Page floating hotel. Other market gunners and fishermen living there at that time were Victor Glodo, Jack Hogg and Fred and Charlie Thomas. She helped with visitors to the hotel and was amazed at the interest the men on the lake had for the Glodo calls. After she and Jack moved to Samburg, they were visited by Ken Anderson who came to Samburg looking for decoys. Jack traded him two Glodo calls for a pressure cooker and some money. Ms. Effe had visited in Glodo's home in Glodo Hollow after he came off the island and knew all of his sons, Jack, Lee (Devior) and Martin, as well as his wife, LaVada.

Odie Quillen and his father, Dan, are both in the picture with Glodo on the porch at Shaw's Store. Odie remembers Glodo from the days when he was a boy fishing for the market with his dad. He remembers Glodo's son, Jack, selling some of his dad's calls for $2.00. (What a deal!) The Glodo's moved from Glodo Hollow into a row of houses on the Old Lake Road, later Hwy 22. Glodo was living here when he died in 1910.

W. C. Gantlett, the Samburg blacksmith, and his wife knew Glodo when they were young. They went to school with the Glodo boys on Chigger Ridge and played with them in their home. W. C. saw Glodo make duck calls using only hand tools. He said there was no room in the house for a lathe and felt he would have noticed it. He said Glodo got the wood smooth by using sand paper and a large piece of glass. Mr. Gantlett said the first person to turn a duck call at

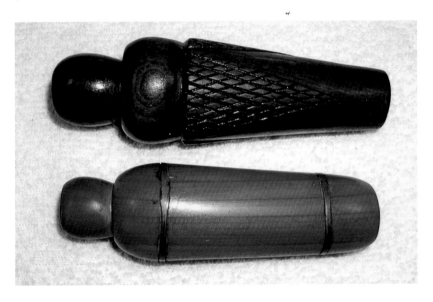

This call set was owned by Charlie Thomas, guide and market hunter who lived on Starve Island with Glodo. The call on the bottom is the only varmint call we have that Glodo made. Note the lead bands used to repair cracks.

Reelfoot was J. E. Cochran. Mr. and Mrs. Gantlett, Mr. and Mrs.Jack Hogg and Dan and Odie Quillen were all at Glodo's funeral at Samburg in 1910, and verify that he is buried in the old Samburg cemetery on the top of the hill behind Ed Hoggs house well above the possible flood water that came thru Reelfoot Lake each spring till the Hickman-Tiptonville levee was built.

THE MAKE-UP OF A VICTOR GLODO, JR. DUCK CALL - Most duck call collectors believe Glodo made two styles of calls. The early calls were made in Illinois with his brothers and in the early years at Reelfoot. They are slimmer, the checkering is narrower and the tone channel is basically the same length but slightly narrower. The end of the insert is opened up to give more volume. All the shoulders on the barrels and most inserts are rounded, giving the great physical appearance we all love. These first calls have been found in the Big Lake Marsh area in Illinois and in the Reelfoot Lake area. There are less than twenty of these with good background information about who had them and where they came from. A lot of the top shot gunners in the area all had Glodos; Guy Ward, Jake Gibbs, John Lykin, P. J. (Babe) Johnson. Most of them knew Glodo.

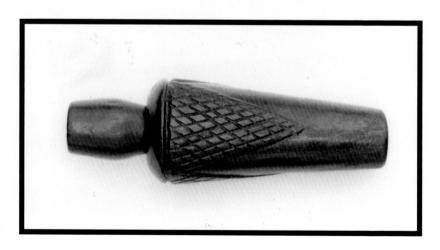

"Hornbeak Glodo" from the Harry Easley collection.

106

These calls were possibly the last calls that Victor Glodo, Jr. made. They belonged to Herman and Ed Dietzel.

The second style of Victor Glodo calls was made after 1900 when Glodo's woodworking skills were diminishing. The wood used was walnut or maple; the checkering is wider and crudely done with the three panels not reaching the base of the call. We have called this skip line checkering because of its width. The tone channel is the same length as the earlier calls and the insert is cored out on the end like the first. There are five or six of these calls in collections; most of them were in the Dietzel family. Mr. Herman Dietzel knew Glodo and Glodo made two of the calls for him and his son Ed. They moved Glodo from the Island to Glodo Hollow (later Dietzel land) and helped him with food and money, as he grew older. Mr. Herman and Ed Dietzel hunted

107

with Glodo and knew his family. These calls are not as valuable as the calls we know as Glodo's first and best, but because of their great look and history, are accredited Victor Glodo's.

As long as the north wind drives flights of mallards south down the Misissippi Flyway each winter, the gunners will hale them with calls made like an old market gunner and king of the jackknife artists made them over one hundred years ago.

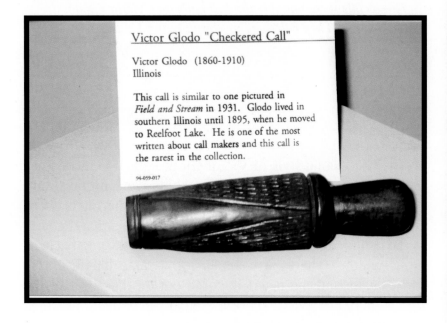

Very rare Victor Glodo call given to the Ward Museum of Wildfowl Art in Salisbury, MD by Howard Harlan.

*Bose Hutchcraft was the original owner
of the Jake Gibbs Glodo. He shot for the
waterfowl market with Glodo in the late 1800's.*

PERRY HOOKER
MASTER DUCK CALL MAKER

Perry Hooker after World War I when he was at his best as a callmaker and shooter.

Perry Hooker (1888-1948), duck call maker and professional target shooter, grew up as a young market hunter in the Iowa and Oklahoma territories where he learned to shoot and make fine duck calls. Perry registered his trap shooting targets as a professional shooter carrying an average of over 95% at the Grand American, home of the ATA in Vandalia, Ohio.

Nash Buckingham, one of Perry Hooker's best pupils, believed Hooker was one of the best callers he ever heard. They hunted together every time Perry was in the Tennessee-Arkansas territory. During World War I, Perry served in England as an airplane engine man, returning to Memphis as often as possible for special duck hunts with Nash Buckingham. This early Hooker history is written about in Nash's story, "The Neglected Duck Call" published in the January, 1928 issue of Field and Stream.

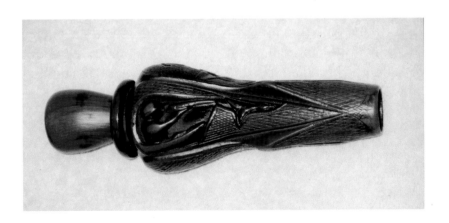

The best Hooker carved duck call.
Note the extended arm of the hunter in the boat.
This call was made in the 1920's.

Hooker came to the Memphis area prior to World War I, about 1912, as a youthful duck hunter and holder of mechanical, automotive, electrical, and marine engineering licenses. During this time he was calling on the hardware and sporting goods trade as a representative of Western Cartridge Company. Perry traveled into Northwest Tennessee to the Reelfoot Lake area, home of the Victor Glodo duck call and other early duck call makers, to live and work. Many times when Perry was the houseguest of Dr. Harvey Marshall of Hornbeak, they hunted on Reelfoot with Reelfoot market hunter and guide, Jack Hogg. They hunted the Grassy Bend area in the "Hogg Hole" at the head of the bend, a spot still hunted by the Hogg family today.

Early calls made by Perry were plain hunting calls with monel metal reeds, some carved or checkered. His inserts show Beckhart influence, and the reeds are squared and tapered with a file. These early calls show more attention to detail; and his carved calls are the best ever made, rivaled only by those of Tom Mays, who carved only two. One of the calls pictured with this article shows a hunter shooting at a duck; note the extended arm, about the width of a toothpick, which has survived over 80 years of handling and hunting.

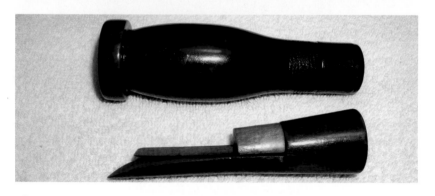

Experimental Arkansas Style

Around 1925 Perry began the development of an Arkansas style call, with a filed rubber reed and a curved insert, for use in the woods. The calls were mentioned in Nash Buckingham's story. Only two of this style call have been found.

Around 1928 when the *Neglected Duck Call* was published, Perry was covered up with orders for his now famous duck calls. During that time Hooker's barrel shape insert changed to look like the Benjon calls. The calls were restyled for production and the quality was not as good. Some of the inserts in this era were stamped "Hooker Duck Call" on the end. Most of the hand carved calls have been found in the West Tennessee area and they are considered the most desirable of all the carved calls.

Hooker lived his later years with his brother-in-law in Memphis where he continued to make a few calls in a basement shop. He later sold his call design and name to Ben Tyler, Bill Day, and John Lorensen. They produced calls under the Benjon Label until the 1950's.

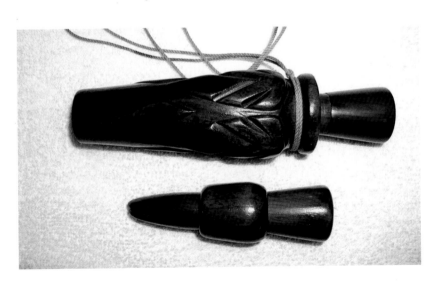

A wonderful pair of calls - duck and crow - made for the Marshall family. The crow call is one-of-a-kind.

It is my belief that Hooker made some of the finest hunting and collector calls ever carved. The dozen or so carved calls we have in collections are "the best of the best." The only other type of call he was known to have made was a one-of-a-kind crow call created as part of a set for Butz Marshall, Dr. Harvey Marshall's son. (The set is pictured with this article.)

This is an early Hooker carved call found in the Reelfoot Lake area.

An interesting piece of research has revealed a meeting in Nash Buckingham's store between Perry Hooker and Tom Turpin. At that time Turpin was a noted turkey call maker who talked with Hooker about developing a duck call. This information helps us date Turpin in the 1928-1930 timetable.

Perry Hooker finished his life in Memphis in 1948 enjoying his hunting buddies and old memories of duckingdays past.

Perry Hooker carved calls vary in price from fifteen to twenty five thousand dollars, depending on the desirability and quality of the call. The regular plain barrel calls are in the thousand to twelve hundred dollar range. There are about twenty carved calls and fifty plain barrel calls in call collections.

*These three duck calls illustrate the
different shapes of Perry Hooker's plain calls.*

*The 1920 Winchester Arms Shooting Squad.
Note Perry Hooker on the right side of this group.*

TOM MAY
(1903 - 1979)
CHAMPION GUNNER
AND DUCK CALL MAKER

TOM MAY

When shotgunners discuss the gunning legends of the old days, Tom May's name always comes up. He was a great duck call maker, but his passion was to hunt and shoot, and he was one of the best. He excelled at all the shotgun games; trap, skeet, and live pigeons. He put his daughter through college with money won in shooting events. When asked what he did for a living, his answer was "I shoot."

Three panels of the
"all time greatest carved call"

Tom taught aerial gunning in the Second World War. He later ran the gun club at Dyersburg, Tennessee for years, instructing hundreds of young shooters in both skeet and trap. My first lesson in skeet came from Tom. He taught using the gun which you hold as a measuring stick for the correct lead. Tom was small of stature, but he was naturally quick and had great eye-hand coordination which helped him to be a great shot. It's said that in the service he had a long run record on skeet targets of 1,214 and many days shot a case of shells for practice.

Tom May started his duck call journey in the mid-forties after the war. At that time he hunted ducks on the Mississippi River and wanted a duck call that would work over a long distance. His first efforts were similar to Turpin's long barrel calls with open-end inserts and deep tone channels, designed to increase volume. He made his own spread of cork decoys, using cork which had been used as insulation in the old icehouse in Dyersburg. A quick river rise floated this spread off. He later made a few carved wooden decoys from pine, a pair of which is pictured here showing his carving skill and attention to detail.

Pair of Tom May's carved mallard decoys
(We have found no more than twelve to fifteen of these.)

Later in his hunting career he made a smaller woods style call with a thinner reed and a raspy sound. It was this style that he made and used in the 1950's and 1960's. I found the little call with the plaited fishing line lanyard in his hunting box. It's one of my favorite calls. His daughter said he kept a rubber band around the insert, reed and wedge to keep them together while soaking them in a glass of water on the windowsill. This way they would be ready to pop into a call barrel for practice.

The two great, carved calls pictured here were made in the 50's when Tom was night manager of the Forked Deer Hotel. They were a gift to his daughter, Julia. When I first took pictures of the calls, I didn't notice the inserts were in the wrong barrels. I later switched them. Each call has three carved panels. Note the detail in the calls pictured. There has never been greater detail and workmanship.

Two carved calls made by May
for his daugher, Julia, in the 1950's.

119

This is folk art at its finest level. I own the box of carving and checkering tools he used to make these calls. His total duck call production was about 150 calls. He never made calls to sell. They were made for friends and for his own personal use.

An interesting story about "Mr. Tom" which was told by his young friend, John Uitendall, of Newbern, Tennessee is as follows: "One day Mr. Tom was hunting on the river south of Ridgley when he found a duck call sticking in the mud. When picking it up, he noticed it was one of three he had made for three skeet-shooting friends. Since he didn't know which one lost it, he penned a short note in each one's Christmas card asking about their call. Two of them replied in glowing phrases about how great their calls were, but the third one reported losing his on the Forked Deer River the year before and how much he missed it." Mr. Tom cleaned the call and returned it to his friend by mail so he could finish the season with it. It was later noted that the call was lost about two miles up river from where it was found.

May's personal duck hunting call
used on the Mississippi River and Reelfoot Lake.

THE HISTORY OF THE COCHRAN FAMILY

*Lakeview Hotel showing John Casewell Cochran
standing on steps. J. E. is just to the right holding the
day's catch with his son - three generations of Cochran men.*

JOHN CASEWELL
"TEDDY" COCHRAN

The Cochran story begins with John Casewell "Teddy" Cochran who came to Reelfoot Lake in the late 1800's and established a hotel for hunters on Starve Island. This location was near the first Union City Hunting Club, Jack Hogg's Camp, Victor Glodo's Camp and Con Young's Camp. Teddy quit hunting in the early 1900's and moved his hotel to Samburg so he could better service his "sports" (city folk who came to hunt and fish).

He was a good promoter and had a full list of guides who took care of hunters and fishermen from all over the country. His hotel is pictured along with three generations of Cochran men. (See accompanying photo.) Teddy was born in Herrin, Illinois and died at age 60 on May 3, 1930. We don't think he made duck calls, but he used the Victor Glodo pictured in Tom Turpin's 1931 "How To Blow A Duck Call" article featured in Field & Stream magazine.

Teddy did make some of the large fishing reels used around the Lake. These were made using the hubs of bicycle wheels and soldering the spokes to the hub for strength. One of the best examples is pictured. (See accompanying photo.) The people on the lake used them faithfully on strong stiff steel rods about three feet long and adhered to the philosophy of pulling and horsing the bass into the boat as quickly as possible to avoid all the underwater obstacles in the lake.

JOHN EVERETT
"SUNDOWN" COCHRAN

John Everett "Sundown" Cochran, son of Teddy Cochran, was born at Reelfoot Lake in 1895. Sundown was the first of the line of Cochran duck call makers carving his first one around 1918. He used the Victor Glodo call as a "go by," and they are similar in design including the three panel checkering patterns, which he worked out with a home-made tool constructed from a pancake turner. Sundown was the first Reelfoot Lake duck call maker to use a lathe. His son tells about him setting up a home-built affair that used a Wisconsin Motor mounted on a sawmill board and used a belt that turned the barrels. The spindle speed was regulated by a cone-shaped spindle that allowed you to reset the belt to speed up or slow the process.

P. L. Jamieson and John "Sundown" Cochran in 1920.
Note Cochran is holding a white coot in his left hand.

All but two of J. E.'s calls were stamped on three sides using a set of steel stamps. J. E.'s daughter, Doris Lanzer, remembers as a little girl stamping the calls one letter at a time then painting each letter with gold paint - "J. E. Cochran, Hornbeak, Tennessee" on the first side, "Reelfoot Lake" on the second side, and "Price - $5.00" on the third.

In addition to his callmaking, Sundown owned a boat dock and powerboat; he served as a guide, and until 1918 he hunted for the market. He used a 16-gauge Winchester pump gun and is remembered as one of the best shots and duck callers on the Lake. Sundown's duck calls are easily identified and second only to Glodo in value. To date, we have located two that are not stamped and about twelve that belong to the Cochran family or duck call collectors. I believe there are a few more out there for collectors; so, "Good Hunting!"

The best J. E. Cochran call located
to date from the collection of Howard Harlan.

124

The short call on the left belonged to guide Tony Wigdor.
The call on the right belonged to Jake Gibbs, a Remington Arms
shooting rep. J. E. Cochran calls have sold for fifteen thousand dollars.

John "Son" Cochran - Premier Reelfoot guide and duck call maker.

JOHN "SON" COCHRAN

John "Son" Cochran was the most productive of the Cochran family call makers. He made over one thousand calls for the public, other guides, and friends. A good business man, he and his wife Bonnie ran a successful restaurant and the best guide service on Reelfoot Lake. He started turning calls around 1940 while in his early 20's. He set up a nice shop with good equipment and would travel to sports shows and demonstrate for the public how to make calls. Son used many different types of wood and had them checkered and decoratively carved at the customer's request. Most of his calls are the same general size and shape. For friends, he made a few smaller ones about the size of the Glodo. He only made metal reed calls. Both his sons, Johnny and Joe, helped him build calls and worked in the guide service.

Custom duck call made by John "Son" Cochran
as a gift to the author (Russell Caldwell) in 1988.

John "Son" Cochran duck calls - some of his best work.

During years when things were slow around the lake, the guides would head north for the summer to work in the sheet metal trade. This is where they learned to build the gunning boxes the lake is noted for, most of them were smaller, fitted with a cushion and served as an extra boat seat.

Cochran sheet-metal shell box and
bicycle-spoke reel. Reel was made around 1890.
Shell box was made as a gift to me in 1989 by "Son" Cochran.

In 1991, Son helped found the Reelfoot lake Waterfowl Festival; and for the last thirteen years the Cochran family has built it into one of the best waterfowl events in the country. It is well attended by hunters and duck call collectors from all over the country and draws over 100 exhibitors and many displays. It is one of the best events of its kind, featuring displays, sales booths, great food, and a sensational duck and goose call contest. Son's wife, Bonnie, passed away this year leaving his daughter Helen Jean and son Johnny as the present day organizers.

J. E. Cochran in his power boat.

CLOYD *"SHARPIE"* SHAW

(1901-1972)
*Sharpie Shaw calling with one of the
big calls in his blind on Reelfoot Lake about 1947.*

CLOYD "SHARPIE" SHAW

The year was 1957, a very different time from today. We had a seventy-day duck season with a four duck limit. There were one hundred million ducks in all the flyways and the Mississippi Flyway was filled with lots of grain and acorn fed mallards. Reelfoot Lake was the place to be for the big duck flights that moved through in December and January. I was a college sophomore with a huge hunting appetite. I guided at my dad's duck camp every weekend and during the month long Christmas holidays. About a week into the holidays, I put a kink in the reed of my loud open water Sharpie Shaw duck call, so to Samburg I went in search of Sharpie for a new reed and retuning. This was my first meeting with one of Reelfoot Lake's legends. Sharpie was a thin, wiry built, happy-go-lucky guy with a lot of personality and inside an hour he had me back on the road with my big call ready for business.

Cloyd "Sharpie" Shaw was born in old Samburg in 1901, the son of John Steel Shaw, the owner of the area where Samburg is now and a one thousand acre farm which extended down the east bank of Reelfoot Lake for several miles. Sharpie had a twin brother named Clyde and they grew up enjoying the little community of Samburg and their father's general store. All of the Shaw boys were good athletes and made the local baseball teams. John Steel Shaw died suddenly in 1910 in a horse and buggy run away accident. After their dad's death the boys had to grow up quickly. Their mother, Paralee, a full blooded Cherokee Indian, had a problem coping after John Steel died, but the family continued to live at the lake on property they inherited from their dad.

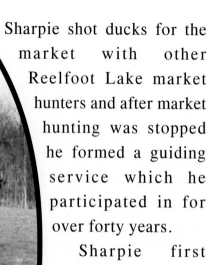

Sharpie shot ducks for the market with other Reelfoot Lake market hunters and after market hunting was stopped he formed a guiding service which he participated in for over forty years.

Sharpie first became interested in duck call manufacturing when he, Elbert Spicer and Kirk Parker went to Memphis to help Tom Turpin tune and develop long range open water duck calls. The time of this adventure was in the early thirties and this started Sharpie on the path of developing his own call. His first efforts were simple as indicated by the duck call he made for his niece's husband, Harold Fowler. The early calls were probably turned on the homemade lathe belonging to J. E. Cochran since it was the only one in Samburg.

A special call with inlays made for John Lykin.

John Lykin, one of Sharpie's best friends and guiding customers, noticed Sharpie's call making efforts. John was a salesman and promoter and became interested in the prospect of helping Sharpie develop and manufacture the calls. Sharpie fitted the calls together and tuned them, John had the parts made, sold and shipped them. The calls were made from the mid thirties until the late fifties. They were advertised in several magazines and John Lykin sold them to sporting goods stores all over the east. The first calls were not the quality of the gold stamped calls, but all the barrels were about the same size and design. The inserts were of at least three different styles but the tone channel, reed, and length are identical.

A stamped Sharpie Shaw call. It was the last call blown by Elbert Spicer, one of Sharpie's market hunting friends.

133

Bob Hilton in Hornbeak, Tennessee and an unknown craftsman in Palmersville, Tennessee made the duck call components. There are between 50 and 100 stamped calls in call collections and the early unstamped are probably numbered at less than 20. This is a hard call to find and purchase from an owner. These calls are very collectable and have traded when found in the thousand dollar range.

Sharpie Shaw left Reefoot Lake in the 1960's to live with his son Claud in Kansas and passed away there May 7, 1972. He lived in the best of times for a waterfowler.

Footnote: A special thanks to Sharon Shaw Fowler Cunningham, Sharpie Shaw's great niece for her historical assistance on Shaw family history and the use of her great family pictures.

*Sharpie as a young man shooting black jacks
from a stump on Rat Island shore on Reelfoot Lake.*

This barrel blind in Forked Pond
was used by Sharpie Shaw and John Lykin
to shoot water turkeys as they passed over in the
1940's. It was a constant irritation to Elbert Spicer
who had the famous Seven Tree Blind in Forked Pond.

JOHNNY MARSH
(1915 - 1983)

Johnny Marsh push-poling a Calhoun
Reelfoot Boat in front of his blind in Katie's Gourd.

JOHNNY MARSH AND LARRY HICKERSON

This is a twofold story about two great Reelfoot Lake duck call makers, their relationship as friends, hunting buddies and finally as teacher and student.

In the beginning Johnny Marsh started making an annual trip to Reelfoot as a part of a Nashville group of duck hunters. The Reelfoot bug bit him and soon he was coming for the whole season taking time away from a Nashville car dealership where he was employed. Johnny was a good fit with the Reelfoot guides and he was welcome with any of them because he had a great personality and had the ability to repair anything.

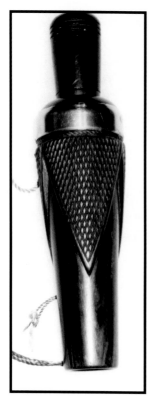

Most of the guides on the lake blew Tom Turpin and Sharpie Shaw calls. After Turpin started *counter* or *step* drilling the barrels, they would stick when blown a lot. Bill Nation, Reelfoot camp owner where Johnny stayed, was having lots of trouble with his Turpin one season in the early 1940's and Johnny declared he could build a call that wouldn't stick. During that off-season was the beginning of the Johnny Marsh Duck Call. The following fall, when Johnny brought those first calls to the lake, they were straight bored, walnut insert, flat top barrel and rounded brass reed, with the famous Johnny Marsh signature written down the side

Johnny Marsh's personal call; his best work.
Note the Glodo relief style checkering.
(From Larry Hickerson's collection)

of the barrel. Johnny and Bill Nation used the first ones and it was said the ducks came for miles to "check in" to those ringing hale calls they blew in Bill's old duck hole off Horse Island ditch. No one can say exactly which season, but because of the lack of "Sports" the camps and guides had access to then, it was just before or during World War II. Later, Johnny Marsh calls had rounded shoulders and the inserts were made from a foreign wood called cocobola. He also built a die for punching out reeds which gave his calls a consistency everyone liked.

Johnny Marsh checkered call used for years by Doris Fraley, Reelfoot guide, Reelfoot's only lady guide. This call is known as a "Two-Finger" Johnny Marsh call made for people with small hands.

In 1949, with Nath Parkerson's help, Johnny built his famous blind in Katie's Gourd and legend says he killed the limit of ducks for three hunters by nine o'clock every day for a seventy-day season.

The quality of Johnny's calls kept improving and he made them out of many different types of wood, with some having high grade gun stock checkering. During the late forties and fifties, he would bring 200 to 300 calls to the lake each fall and sell them over the season. Some seasons he "batched" with his friend Nath Parkerson, but his eventual lake home became Cabin 1 at Bill Nation's Camp. Each evening the festivities were hunters gathering there for drinks and tall stories. He became a hero for literally hundreds of hunters, both young and old. "He had one of the most magnetic personalities of anyone I have ever known," said his friend, Ron DeBerry.

Johnny built a large passenger boat with a car engine that was used to ferry hunters across the open water. It also had a steel plate on the bow, which made it a great ice breaker. He towed Calhoun boats behind it for the hunters to use. I remember those bitter January days with Johnny's big boat breaking 4 inch thick ice and everyone following behind him across the lake to the hunting area. He was the **man!**

Johnny and Tom May were the only Reelfoot Lake duck call makers who made decoys, some of which are pictured here. Johnny made a great set of cork coot decoys for confidence decoys. He and his friend, Joe Foxall, made stools of styrofoam decoys with "Decoys Unlimited" molds each year. These all had the J. M. brand on the bottom and molded weights for stability. They later developed a method of gluing burlap to the decoy bodies, making them super strong. Each year they hand painted the spread and the decoys surely looked real when they were on the water. Johnny was not only a great duck caller, but he worked harder on his equipment than most hunters. To him it was a year-round project. He had his own duck call instruction tape. Johnny even made a stock for his Winchester Model 12. His friend, Phillip Crowe, did a painting of him on Reelfoot Lake in his Calhoun Lake Boat.

Larry Hickerson standing on the lake bank at
Kirby's Pocket blowing Johnny Marsh's personal duck call.

Everyone loved and respected Johnny, especially **Larry Hickerson,** who became Johnny's heir apparent to the big duck call. In the late 1970's and early 1980's, Larry became Johnny's pupil in the duck call business and they developed an almost father-son relationship. They hunted and fished everywhere together; made calls, shot teal, clay targets and doves. It was a special time for both of them. In Larry's book, "It Seemed Like the Thing to Do", he tells many great stories of duck hunts Johnny had with Nash Buckingham and Carl Perkins.

Larry Hickerson wrote some great stories in his book. Some of his descriptions bring back a flood of memories for older hunters. In his story "Charcoal and Propane" some of the opening lines are classics. "Johnny Marsh often told me of duck hunting from makeshift blinds made by sticking a few canes around the boat and no heat. It was suffering in its purest form. Every duck hunter from that period in time remembers the smudged faces, singed hair, and headaches from hell brought on by huddling around the charcoal bucket trying to warm up before the next flight of ducks is spotted." Great stuff!

Larry Hickerson's personal duck call.

Larry had developed a full line of hunting calls for his company; a plastic reed Arkansas style duck call, a goose call and a turkey box call, but his favorite is the old metal reed. He, his family and friend Joe Foxall still enjoy Reelfoot duck hunting each year in their blind off Coot Slough using some of Johnny's old blocks and metal reed calls, cooking up "Go Downs", working the birds and telling the old stories of times past.

A special thanks to Larry Hickerson for his stories, pictures and duck call information.

Johnny Marsh's cork coot decoy - one of one
hundred that he made and used for thirty years in Katie's Gourd.
(1950-1980)

TOM TURPIN
A HALF CENTURY QUEST FOR
GAME CALL PERFECTION
BY HARRY EASLEY

Tom Turpin goose hunting on Mississippi River in 1948.

INTRODUCTION

It's with much pleasure that I introduce my guest writer, my friend and fellow duck call collector Harry Easley. Harry and I started our collecting journey together in the early 1960's and we both loved the old brown Reelfoot Lake calls best, especially Turpins. Many times I would run a duck call lead down and find Easley had been there first. We both loved the Turpin calls, I guess because before Sharpie Shaw and Johnny Marsh all the Reelfoot Lake Guides and hunters blew Turpins and they favored the straight bores. The following article covers Turpin with great information and affection. Thanks Harry.

If there is ever a Game Call Maker's Hall of Fame Tom Turpin should surely be a worthy candidate for early induction. Mr. Tom Turpin produced quality wild game calls in a shop behind his home at 1150 Eastmoreland Avenue, Memphis, TN from around 1900 until approximately 1952. He was an avid hunter and fervently desired that the hunter who used his calls would be successful. To this end he wrote very detailed instructions on how to use his calls, which he typed and sent to his customers along with the call.

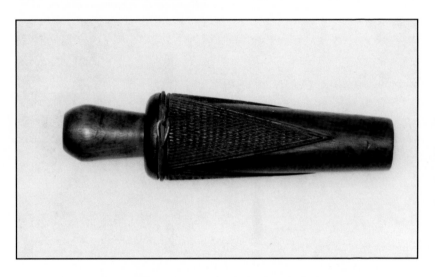

The "Best of the Best" Turpin with raised checkering.
From the collection of Harry Easley.

What may set Tom Turpin apart from his contemporaries and many later call makers was his almost obsessive efforts to improve his calls. He hunted with noted guides from Minnesota to Louisiana, studied their calling methods and sought their advice. He strove to make a call his customer would consider "the best caller on earth" and one that would last a lifetime.

Turpin made calls for around 50 years (nearly 60 years if we are to believe Mr. J. L. Melancon to whom his business was sold in 1956 by his heirs. The Melancon business was later sold to David Tucker, Jonesboro, LA.) During this time he experimented with many reed materials, including nickel, brass, German silver, rubber, and silver plate. Eventually he rejected all these and chose to use reeds made of bronze or "hardened copper".

Teak was his wood of choice for the duck call wedge blocks and stoppers. He had made duck calls of bakelite, hard rubber and various kinds of wood, both domestic and imported. The man-made materials weren't acceptable to him because they didn't produce the "soft" tone he desired in a duck call. Calls with bakelite barrels reportedly produced a satisfactory sound, but Turpin ceased production of these because when dropped overboard they immediately sank. He stated that "teak would not crack, split, change shape, nor swell but little when saturated"; qualities he did not find a domestic wood to possess.

The Turpin duck calls were modeled after the famous Glodo duck call which Turpin considered the best general purpose duck call he had ever used. He felt he had greatly improved on the Glodo call by using a foreign wood for stoppers and wedges, which would not swell, crack or otherwise change shape when wet. In his "Standard Instructions" he stated, "My reed has the tone quality of Glodo's best calls but is of a harder material that will not get out of tune so readily and, if taken care of, should last a lifetime."

One innovation some attribute to Tom Turpin is undercutting, or overboring, the middle part of the inside of a duck call barrel until it is larger than the mouthpiece or where the insert enters the barrel. J. L. Melancon wrote that this characteristic was begun by Turpin, working in conjunction with Victor Glodo. The story went that the sound in the dome shaped bottom of a dug well was louder than that in the well shaft; therefore, creating a larger diameter in the middle of a duck call barrel would make the call louder. There were dissenting opinions, however. Elbert Spicer, who blew a "straight bored" 3 duck Turpin call once told me that the back boring was something the Memphis sports talked Turpin into doing and that all it was good for was a spit trap. One thing is certain - Turpin made some calls that were straight bored and some "Glodoed".

Turpin Open Water and Woods set with one insert.

Judging from his writing and ads, the call that evolved as Turpin's "bread and butter" duck call was his large open water call. They were made with an insert of teak and a walnut barrel. He offered a "deluxe" model with a barrel of teak or burl walnut. If his customer desired a lower volume call for timber hunting he offered a shorter barrel "timber" call; or he supplied a call with two barrels - one timber and the other open water. In later years he stamped flying ducks on his barrels, probably to distinguish them from his imitators. Usually he stamped 3 ducks on his standard open water calls but ordinarily none on his timber calls.

During his tenure as a game call maker Turpin produced a variety of products. His book <u>Ducks - How to Call Them</u>, published in 1932, lists the following items for sale: turkey calls, crow calls, squirrel calls, a one-piece shotgun-cleaning rod and phonograph records. In addition to his duck calling records he marketed records of turkey calling and crow calling. His duck calling records featured calling by noted callers of the time, including Elbert Spicer of Reelfoot lake fame. Also there were hawk and varmint calls produced that were attributed to him. In 1951 he sold the crow call and crow call record business to W. I. Turpin, Sr. (Inman).

Turpin crow call, a gift from Emery Burden to Russell Caldwell, has seen 40 years of successful crow hunting.

Tom Turpin in 1913.

Although my interest in him has been primarily as a maker of duck calls, he probably was equally famous as an early turkey call maker. He produced box calls, yelpers made of wing bone, reed, coco bola and a hybrid combination with a wood barrel and bone, which he called a tree yelper.

Possibly one facet about Turpin that is not widely known is that he was a very early game call collector. In a Memphis newspaper article, authored by Frank Vestal, there is a picture of the Turpin collection. In the picture are identified calls by G. D. Kinney, J. E. Cochran, Fafer,

"Slingshot Charlie" Taylor and others, including a Cajun call which was a gift from Mr. E. A. McIlhenny (of Avery Island/Tabasco hot sauce fame). The author stated that the calls had been gathered by Mr. Turpin over a long period of years.

The game call business, which Tom Turpin started, was continued by his brother W. Inman Turpin, Sr. and Inman's son, Hunter Turpin. Now Hunter Turpin's son, Steve Turpin, continues the tradition by producing game calls at his home, 4911 Essexshire, Memphis, TN 38117. The author is indebted to him for some of the information and pictures of Tom Turpin used in this article.

Crow call made by Inman Turpin. (Ray Terrell Collection)

Teak Deluxe Duck Call. (Harry Easley Collection)

CONTEMPORARY CALL MAKERS

TERRY NORRIS

The best of the contemporary duck call makers and carvers.
His work is always rewarded at the shows with a top finish.
His duck calls and goose calls do a good job in the duck blind.

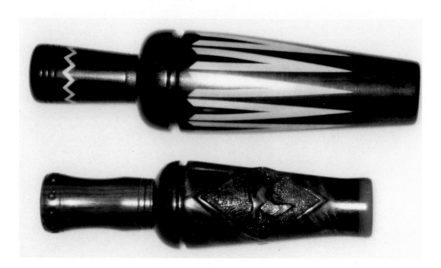

EMERY BURDEN

*A great duck call maker and a best friend.
Emery and I have shot all over the country; crows,
ducks, doves, clay targets, turkeys and pigeons, and I
can honestly say he is the best hunter I have ever hunted
with and the best all-around shot. We have hunted crows
together for over 45 years and together killed over forty
thousand up and down the Mississippi River.*

MARK PIERCE

Robert Caldwell and Mark Pierce duck call maker and guide.
Successfully guides hunting parties from all over the United States.

J. D. DOWNING

Business man and duck call maker.
Owns Lakeview Dining Room.

BILLY RICHARDSON

Fisherman and duck call maker.

CHARLES AND MAC DIETZEL

*The last living member of the Union City Hunting Club.
He has a lot of knowledge of the early Reelfoot
years and information about Victor Glodo, Jr.*

SHAWN TANKERSLEY

Peter Lawrence, Rob Caldwell, and Shawn Tankersley who is one of the best craftsmen on the lake. We have enjoyed some special times together.

SUCCESS JOURNEYS

Russell and Donna Caldwell

THE SUCCESSFUL AND HAPPY LIFE

As I reflect and look back at my goals and life experiences, I ponder what makes life successful and happy for some and a failure for others. I believe that there are a few keys for the successful and they follow:

The most important decision a successful and happy person makes is the acceptance of Christ as Savior.

The greatest power a successful person uses well, is the power of choice. The successful well-rounded person will make correct choices about all of life's opportunities, career, a lifetime mate, hobbies. He will choose things he can learn to do for a long period of time and will make a commitment to doing them all with enthusiasm. He will not fear change; it is the order of life.

The common denominator that the successful person has is good habits; he will commit himself to forming these because they make him happy and positive results give success.

The most important trait a successful and happy person has is persistence. This trait will keep you from quitting when you are close to winning or accomplishing the job or task.

Many times, the distance you go in life has to do with the setting of goals. There are two types of goals, long term and immediate. Be sure and commit all goals to writing in a journal or log book. When ones goals become a picture of reality in the mind it will help motivate one to determined action.

Remember, that the successful Christian life is a journey of many steps and our destination is a wonderful afterlife with our Lord, so enjoy life's successes and opportunities as they come. Devote yourself to loving others and creating a life that gives you purpose and meaning. Always bless others.

Russell H. Caldwell

John L. Warner

SUCCESSFUL LIVING

Success in life is a journey not a destination. As you make the successful journey you experience the essence of life. Worthwhile achievements are accomplished incrementally, one step at a time. Journeys are best enjoyed in fellowship with others.

Begin each day in fellowship with God. Learn of Him through His Word. Open your heart to Him in prayer. Listen intently for His response to your pleas. Observe carefully His work in His universe as you walk through it. Remember that every person is a special child of God, made in His image, worthy of your love and respect.

Develop a God like character. Have a unified personality exemplified by integrity. Forgive others as you also need forgiveness. Keep short accounts. Don't let the sun go down on your anger. Be loving and kind rather than judgmental. Try to put yourself in the other person's shoes. Have a sense of humor. Think of elephants, giraffes, zebras. Discover principles, identify people for whom you would be willing to die. At the same time pick your battles carefully. Correct most of your own mistakes, but only correct others when it really matters. Even when you are in a teaching role, correct gently. Let your love of the student be far more evident than your love of truth. Fully experience joy and sorrow and know that the joy shared is double joy while the sorrow shared is only half sorrow. Develop patience. Remember how longsuffering God has been with you. Approach each day, each challenge, each opportunity, with a spirit of adventure, eager to let God teach you something new. Remember the tortoise and the hare. Both had to get going. Pace yourself so you'll finish the race. Think. Be steady. Be willing to make the extra effort that distinguishes excellence from mediocrity. Don't forget for Whom you labor.

161

See yourself as a steward. Each day of life is a gift from God. Use it as a responsible steward. Each possession you have is on loan from God. Care for it as you would a library book. Be a steward of your body so you can be of better service. Each person you meet intersects your life to enrich your life or his or both of your lives. Respond responsibly. Learn to distinguish distractions from God's appointments which you didn't anticipate. Be flexible. Adapt to change, remember, you don't possess things, they possess you. Accordingly, consider each possession as God's property placed in your care.

Some situations in life are what I call tar babies. The sooner you can escape, the better off you'll be. If you fight with a tar baby, you'll end up getting stuck, thereby losing opportunities to help others.

Know what is within your boundaries and what is not. Ultimately, your boundary ends with your skin. People, events outside your boundaries are beyond your control. Accept it.

Because life is so fleeting, maximize the amount of time you spend in communion with those for whom you are responsible: spouse, offspring, ancestors, siblings, friends, fellow workers, fellow worshippers. At the same time, reserve time to reach out and expand your circle of concern.

Be balanced. Be patient, even as God is patient with you. Love your spouse. This is the greatest gift you can give to your child.

John L. Warner

Photography courtesy of Donna Caldwell

Robert E. Kirkland

ACHIEVING SUCCESS

First, how to achieve it.

You better do something with your life that you enjoy. I can think of nothing worse than to work at something that you dislike. If you work at something you like, you'll never work another day of your life. This is for success in life and happiness, but not financial success.

Be well read, whether you're well educated or not. Books are cheap. They teach the thoughts of the greatest thinkers in history. If you can't afford a book, go to the library. Important choices arise every day, choices that can be life changing. Chances are better that you will make the right choice if you are well informed.

Being selfish is a must. I know, I know, all your life you have been told that being selfish is wrong, that you should sacrifice for your parents, spouse, children or someone or something. Not true. You'll only end up being unhappy. A key measure of success is happiness and you can't be happy or successful if you feel miserable, disappointed and guilty most of the time.

Next, you must have a philosophical or religious base on which to base your decisions - a standard by which to absolutely judge right from wrong. Discover the virtues that have been beneficial throughout history, learn about them and live by them (Back to reading. See point 2 above). None of this relativist morality junk. None of the thought that it is wrong to murder, but sometimes it's OK. Absolute concepts are not only possible but also necessary for success.

Know yourself. All of us have strengths and weaknesses. If you don't distinguish between them, you will forever be frustrated and unhappy. Success cannot follow a person who hasn't explored their own psyche.

Don't believe all of what you've been taught, believe little of what you've read or seen on TV, and believe just some of what you've seen first-hand. Don't unconditionally accept the beliefs of "experts."

Moral: Don't live afraid. Don't believe the scare headlines.

Life's success comes from the above stuff. That's how to achieve it.

But what change will success in life make in you? You will be happy and without guilt, a proud individual, standing tall, confident in your life and possess a positive view of yourself. You will have earned self-esteem.

And what does it boil down to? What is success in life? Here's my belief. Big drum roll please.

If you can reach the age of 65 and still have your sanity with all the baloney, misrepresentations and outright lies thrown at you all the previous years of your life, you will be a success in life."

Thought of the Week: "As it has been said before, he has achieved success who has lived well, laughed often and loved much, who has accomplished his task, whose life is an inspiration and whose memory a benediction."

Robert E. Kirkland

Tom and Sherry Hendrix

SUCCESS THROUGH SERVICE

Life is a bit like getting into an automobile at night and turning on the headlights. They don't shine all the way home. They shine to the bottom of the hill. When you get to the bottom of the hill, they shine to the top. Through faith, we believe the road will take us home. It's the same with life. Our lights, simply, don't shine all the way.

Upon graduation from college, we see our first project and not much further. God must have known what he was doing when he made sure we could not see all of life in the beginning but see it one piece at a time so we could completely concentrate on that project, gaining some experience, broadening our vision to see a bit further.

There is too much emphasis placed on making a living or joining a company with a good benefit package for early retirement. In my opinion, there is too much focus on what I can get instead of what I can contribute. The Bible does not speak of an individual reaching a point, regardless of age, where they are commissioned to occupy the stool of "do nothing" - where they cease to contribute to society. This may be the reason why there is not a retirement chapter in the New Testament. This attitude of making a living, retire as soon as you get enough money, can stunt your growth.

Life should be a mission of service...something we are willing to give our life for. All we have in this life is X amount of time and when we give time to something, we are simply exchanging a part of our life for it. If we think our life is special, our mission should be just as special. We can't help but feel passionate about our work if it is our mission, something we are willing to give our life to and having deep feelings about our work is completely essential for success. Enthusiasm comes from the way we feel. If we feel strongly about our work, our mission, we can't help but be enthusiastic and nothing great was ever accomplished without enthusiasm. The original Greek meaning of enthusiasm is "the God within". When we fully comprehend that God is within us, we approach life with a confidence, awe inspired, energetic, optimistic and service minded attitude. We truly embody enthusiasm. If we can choose our mission, within our natural gifts, we will do it better and enjoy it more.

Education is not just "book learning". It is being a student of life - all aspects of it - with knowledge of human nature and how to deal with people. Education helps us better understand our universe and how it works. We should see the practical aspect of our education, understanding we can get what we want by simply helping others get what they want. This is an obvious truth but many times overlooked which explains why a lot of people don't realize their dreams, become frustrated and don't understand why they are not making more progress. Everyone has an equal shot at success, but we must comply with the rules of success to get there. I don't think God is in the business of selecting one person to be successful and one to fail. We must understand, "if it's to be, it's up to me".

Success is more an attitude, some people have it and some do not. This successful attitude enables us to effectively use a greater percentage of what we know. Education, on the other hand, is just information unless we can use it for someone's benefit. (Example - Dr. Salk's polio vaccine) This certain success attitude helps us put our education to work for good, to have anything we want within reason. In many cases, we do not understand the power of faith, service, integrity, generosity, love, and the great moral truths that Christ taught for a successful, happy life.

Success is an inside job. It's becoming the person we should become in life. If we believe we are created in the image of God, and I do, we were meant to be special and achieve great goals. God did not want us to be poor with a downtrodden feeling. Being created in the image of God is to be a winner!

Whether we are teachers, preachers or businessmen, we should have a positive attitude toward money because so many of our activities involve money. Money should not be the goal. Service is the goal and we should not get the two confused. If money is the goal, we are apt to cut corners, sacrificing our values to achieve it. If we sacrifice our values, we sacrifice our happiness and effectiveness. That is a lose - lose situation! Money should be viewed as a tool in the tool chest like a hammer or saw. We should guard against having an emotional attachment to money. Some people are so afraid that they will lose their money they never use it, and therefore their money ceases to be a tool reverting back to a goal. People like money for what it can do for them; I have never had a payroll check returned. Money gives an extra measure of freedom - families can take that wonderful family vacation, send their children to a school of their choice, build a dream home they have always wanted, and the list goes on and on. No one wants to limit himself or herself or their good ideas with *I can't afford it.* It seems to me our money goals should be to become financially free through service to others. We get money, for the most part, one of three ways. You can break the law and steal it and end up in jail. You can inherit money and that's wonderful because it was left to you with love. Celebrate it all the way to the bank - just use it for good. However, rendering service to our fellowman, is mostly, how we acquire our money. A teacher who nudges children in the right direction, receives a check at the end of the month for services rendered. There is nothing wrong in becoming a multimillionaire in service to others and we should never feel guilty. Simply celebrate the service trip. Doing something special for others is the best way I know to express our love to our fellowmen. We should kick up our heels in service to others. It is the most productive and happiest way to live.

171

The profit motive is criticized for being greedy. Profit to a business is as necessary as food is to a child - both have to have it to live. It is essential that companies earn a profit for their employee's job security and the best way to earn a profit is to focus on good service. There is a built-in pruning device in our free enterprise system that prunes off those who fail to serve. A greedy businessperson will not do well over time because his service will reflect his attitude. The people in a neighborhood make choices every day regarding what businesses they are going to support. It is not a bad system when people decide who will serve them. In a free society, we call it people power.

There is a plan for mankind. The plan grows and evolves through the centuries as does any flower, tree or other living thing according to the immutable laws of God that govern the universe. Man determines his own fate by the degree to which he cooperates or opposes the will of the Creator operating the plan. Our goal should be to grow toward God through service to our fellowman.

I will close with a thought from my good friend, Jack McConnico. Jack died at the age of seventy-four and gave his body to science. I asked him why he planned this course of action and Jack replied, "I am going to render service to my fellowman as long as I shall live and at my death maybe the scientific research community can use my body to cure an illness or disease. That is my way of getting full measure out of Jack McConnico." In my opinion, Jack understood how to live - the significance of expressing his life through service to others.

Thomas E. Hendrix

Photograph courtesy of R. C. Owen

Carl Kirkland

QUALITIES OF SUCCESSFUL PEOPLE

Most of the successful people I have known are:

- More determined than most
- Always self-starters
- Smart enough, but typically not exceptionally smart
- Willing to do what others are not willing to do
- Lot of common sense or "street smarts" instead of book smarts
- Do not over analyze
- Usually operate on business parameters that are calculations that can be done in one's head. An example: In bidding a contract they typically can tell you quickly what a job will cost based on bench marks developed from experience.
- Do not dwell on mistakes
- Confident, deservedly or not
- Do not fear failure or even consider it or have a poorly developed sense of fear
- They are impatient and achieve more because they are persistant.
- Sometimes have no concept of the odds against them

Success is often determined to mean financial success, but obviously there are many other perhaps more important definitions of success. The only meaningful measure of success is what you are doing compared to your potential. In my personal case, it's not that I am smart, but I would propose that I may be more determined than most.

Happiness is an even more difficult subject. The happiest people I have known do not seem to correspond with the most successful list. The happiest people are those that live unselfishly. They do a lot to help others. They do not dwell on thinking about themselves. Few people learn this early enough in life. Some of the most lost people I know lacked a purpose other than money. To be happy, try to make others happy, have a spiritual side to your life, respect others truly and show it.

Carl Kirkland

Photograph by Donna Caldwell

Caleb L. Davis III, Wade Mansfield, Dr. "Chubby" Andrews

OUR CULTURE

Since the beginning of human existance, men who liked to hunt and fish and who loved the out-of-doors have come together.

In modern history, this culture has grown and been re-fined. Today it exemplifies the finest traits of the human race. Today the people who hunt and fish do it not only for what they harvest but also for the experience of being out in God's great masterpiece - nature.

As I look back on the wonderful road of my life, invaribly some of the greatest moments have been those I experienced in the out-of-doors. Likewise many of my greatest relationships came from my outdoor activities.

I made it a priority to see that my children had a chance to experience the wonderful creations that I have. I also tried to instill in them the idea that it is their responsibility to pass this culture on to their children.

This wonderful outdoor culture is the greatest legacy we can leave for the generations that come behind us.

God gave us dominion over nature but he also gave us the responsibility of preserving it.

Caleb L. Davis III

Robert E. Clendenin, Jr.

ROBERT E. CLENDENIN, M. D.
2211 WEDGEWOOD DRIVE
UNION CITY, TENNESSEE 38261

I don't think that there are any mysterious secrets about achieving success and happiness.

It helps to have parents and family to start you off with a strong work ethic, character and a sense of right and wrong. At times others, such as your Pastor, a special teacher or various community leaders may provide this help.

You must have goals in life and you have to be willing to work hard to achieve them. There will be obstacles along the way and you must work to overcome them. Each time you are knocked down get back up and keep going. You are not defeated until you stay down.

It helps to be comfortable with yourself. I think that having a strong Religious background helps you accomplish this. Being comfortable with who you are provides ballast for the stormy parts of life.

Also deal with things in life as they are, not as you fantasize them to be.

Then if you are fortunate to find a partner in life with the same ideals and goals that you have you are poised to have success and happiness in all aspects of life — work, home and family.

Robert E. Clendenin Jr.

1952 Northwest Conference Champions "Point-a-Minute-Team...having made 432 points in 432 minutes of regular playing time. It is hoped that many of these players can be at Homecoming on October 18, 1974. They are [left to right] Top Row- Jack Lambert, Coach;Eloiett Johnson, Lewis Sewell, Joe Marvin Goss, Leon Milligan, Buddy Miller, Jere Stripling, Jack Pate, William Murray and Marion Carrell, Ass't Coach; Middle Row- Robert Gerald Burkett, Robert Sewell, Jon Stripling, Joe Akin, Jimmy Gibbons, Jimmy Roney, Jimmy Wilson, Donald Pitt; Bottom Row- Walter Rainey, Eugene Ring, Charles McKnight, John Gordon Rudolph, Bill Leonard and James Ingram.

Dr. "Chubby" Andrews, Russell Caldwell and Jere Stripling

THE POINT A MINUTE TEAM

Adlai Stevenson said, "If you compare yourself with others, you may become vain or bitter; for there will always be those persons lesser or greater than yourself" - - Good advice, especially when you have friends like Donna and Russell Caldwell.

I was, however, privileged to be a member of one incomparable group. The 1952 Newbern, Tennessee High School football team scored exactly 432 points in 432 minutes of regular season play and was described in "Ripley's Believe It or Not," as "The Point A Minute Team." The believe it or not part is not the volume of scoring that was accomplished; for many teams on all levels of competition have scored more than a point a minute. The trick was to hit it on the nose and we didn't realize that this had happened until weeks after the season had ended. In the early eighties, the American Football Coaches' Association had an article in their newsletter about high scoring teams and came up with no team, other than Newbern that had scored exactly a point a minute.

The point-a-minute, however, is not what makes this story a candidate for Russell's book. There were things happening to this team that were far more important than touchdowns and shutouts.

Now, Newbern is not a mega-metropolis and there were only thirteen boys in that senior class in 1952. We didn't have a town square. We had a triangle. When I went to Memphis for my physical to determine my draft status, 23 other Dyer County lads with similar birthdays accompanied me. I think we were a pretty good cross-section of white, twenty-year-olds from our area. Eight of the group had not finished the eighth grade and needed help in reading the required forms. Eight more had not finished high school. Two were in college at the time.

Thirteen boys played in the games that season in 1952 until victory was assured. From those thirteen there developed three doctors, three coaches, a veterinarian, a minister, a missile base mathematician and a farmer with a degree in agriculture. The three who chose to work instead of seeking a college degree all had successful careers and are enjoying a comfortable retirement.

The last fifteen years of my career were spent traveling the country, looking at college football players to determine their prospects of playing professionally. There are some long, lonesome roads in Texas, Oklahoma, Washington and Wyoming. I've passed a lot of hours trying to determine what made our group special. Why, in an environment in which the average male did not finish high school, did this group of thirteen guys get ten college diplomas and eight degrees beyond a Bachelor's?

At the core was a bright, hardnosed, demanding coach, who was a Naval Officer in the Pacific during World War II. He wore the hero's mantle with great naturalness. His wife taught typing and tried to make us realize that life existed outside of West Tennessee. His assistants were far more interested in our well-being than their own.

Our Principal was a World War II veteran who made the ground shake when he came close. Paddle whacks originating from his office could be heard in all parts of the building. Those of us who had been some closer to the action on past occasions would break into a cold sweat.

All of our summers were spent around adults - sometimes fathers - sometimes merchants - sometimes a local farmer. Each church had a youth choir and a director with the patience of Job. Each church also had an active youth fellowship organization and Sunday afternoon trips to regional gatherings were routine. I must have attended fifty banquets and progressive dinners from the eighth grade through high school.

When a number of businessmen heard that some of my older brother's group were having trouble with room and board at college, they bought an old school bus and ran a daily shuttle to Martin Junior College, forty miles away. A farmer loaned the school part of his irrigation system so that we could get a sod started on our game field before the '52 season. The Governor attended our opening game and dedicated a new city fire truck. Someone saw to it that we got to see the Memphis Chicks, St. Louis Cardinals, The Bears vs. Redskins in a Memphis Exhibition Game (Lojack and Baugh), the Delta Bowl (Jack Cloud), Kentucky's Fabulous Five (Beard and Groza) against Ole Miss. The entire squad attended the '53 Cotton Bowl and the '54 Sugar Bowl.

My family didn't own a car, so some member of the community saw to it that we were exposed to a lot of fine people and many great events. I'm extremely thankful that I grew up in a community where education was important, parents were involved and kids knew what was expected of them. It might be that Hillary is on to something. Maybe it does take a village. Thank you Newbern!

Jere Stripling

CALDWELL FAMILY BUSINESS JOURNEY WITH UNION CITY AND SURROUNDING AREA

In 1820 James Caldwell moved to this area clearing land and establishing farming interest to serve the food needs of area people. Later his son, David P. Caldwell, continued to farm and built a toll road across the Obion River east of Union City on the Dresden-Hickman road, thus becoming the first Caldwell businessman to serve our area.

D. P. Caldwell, Jr. moved into Union City in its beginning and established Caldwell's Book Store on First Street in 1891. In addition to selling school books to the city and county students, he furnished office supplies such as stationery, ledgers and files, along with Bibles and other reading materials. D. P., Jr. helped establish the Union City Training School, a private school, to help prepare local students for college. During the 1920's he served in the State Legislature at the same time his brother, William Caldwell, served the 8th Congressional District in Congress in Washington, D. C.

D. P., Jr.'s son and my dad, Chester W. Caldwell, took over Caldwell's Book Store in 1928 after D. P.'s death. He moved the store farther south to 223 South First Street close to the Farmers Exchange Bank on part of the Verhine property. The name was changed to Caldwell's Store and he added several more items for sale such as typewriters, sporting goods, hardware, housewares, paint, wallpaper, novelties and a candy counter. I started my career in this business, first as a stock boy, typewriter repairman, and last as an office supply salesman while I was in college at U. T. Martin. Dad sold the store to the Kirkland family in the late 1950s right after our 100th year celebration of Union City.

When my wife, Donna Hauser, and I married in July 1960, we started a business journey together that to date has lasted 45 years. We started Caldwell's Office Outfitters in a small warehouse on Depot Street, and as we grew we moved into a garage on North Fifth Street. We sold office supplies and I worked on typewriters at night. Donna ran the office in the day time and worked as an RN on the 3 to 11 shift at Obion Co. General Hospital. Our first formal location was a converted house on Hwy 45 W. at the site of our present building which was built in 1971. We evolved into office equipment and furniture, furnishing the new Obion County High School and several of the new buildings on the U. T. Martin campus. Our printing operation was started in 1966 and the first pressman was a college student by the name of Art Bond. After graduation from U.T., he came to work for us full time and is now a Vice President in the company. He has seen tremendous changes in our industry and has continued to grow and help service our customer base in West Tennessee and Kentucky.

In 1987 our direction changed again and we added the copier and leasing business including our son, Harold. Harold established a coin operated copier business and leasing company, HRC Rentals, that handles leases for the Caldwell's Office Outfitters customer base to this day. A growth spurt in the 1980's brought other members of our family into the business. Our daughter, Patricia, established the Graphic Arts Department for our print shop, and our daughter, DeLise, helped set up the Service Department for the copier division.

Due to the tremendous growth in the Jackson, Tennessee area, we opened a branch office there in 1992 with our son, Robert, being in charge of setting it up and running it. Donna and I, in that same year, set up another leasing company, Caldwell's Leasing, to take care of the growth in the Jackson area. Our desire to service our customers completely has allowed us tremendous opportunities and blessings. We cover all of West Tennessee except the Memphis area with twenty eight employees and three locations. Our history has paralleled that of Union City, one of service to the environment and the people of the area. We at Caldwell's feel great about the future of our company and our town. Six generations of Caldwells have been involved in the business community of Union City and have contributed to the continued growth of the area with service and good will to the community and its people.

D. P. CALDWELL'S BOOK STORE.

MENTORS

This section of my book is about the men who had an impact on my life with their presence and interest. I think you never quit changing and it is important to have mentors, role models, people you can use as a model to base your life on. The great thing about these men is that they were all Christians with deep seated Bible based values. Two helped to mold me as a young person and three as a man.

Chester Caldwell

CHESTER

In every duck hunter's life there is usually an old hunter who passes on the heritage and lore that means so much to them. When I take my yearly trip down memory lane, my friend Chester comes to mind.

I remember my first duck hunt with him...I couldn't have been over seven or eight years old. As I close my eyes I feel the wind in my face as he rowed our boat toward the hole off the ditch in Goose Pocket. I can still see those first ducks that came in before shooting time in that half light all hunters know so well. I pleaded with him to go ahead and shoot them early, but Chester held firm and those precious minutes ticked by until it was okay to shoot. I can still feel the thrill of that first duck and how proud I felt even though it was sitting on the water for the first shot.

I remember helping with our first blind. Chester was a professional "make do" fellow, so it was not the art form we shoot out of today. Man, it was cold on a north wind! That crack around the big cypress tree was just like having the door open! I remember paper shells that swelled, wooden decoys that rocked in the water, Reelfoot Lake rowboats that leaked, and charcoal buckets that smoked your eyes until they got going. Through all of this, Chester shared his knowledge and patience with me. I can still hear him correct me for stopping my swing on a fast Black Jack or calling too hard on an old greenhead that was going to work anyway.

Chester had an old cabin that was his duck camp on Upper Blue Basin and he had a blind off Mud Basin in open water. He shot a Nickel Steel Model 12 in the early days and always blew an Earl Dennison call. He shot with the old timers for the market when he was a boy and would get that faraway look in his eyes when he talked about the clouds of ducks that used the lake between 1918 and 1929. He shot clay targets with Jake Gibbs and Babe Johnson and quit the day he reached his goal of 25 straight.

Most of Chester's friends were old hunters and they were at their best telling those old tales I loved to hear. In the front room of the cabin, around the potbelly stove, "H." Whipple or Big George Lee would take the floor and the tales they told were of a hunting time that a young man could only dream about. Can you imagine shooting a case of shells in a day and bringing in over a hundred ducks, or having the opportunity of shooting one specie of ducks for a day and not fooling with any trash ducks?

As Chester grew older, it became more important to teach and share than to kill. Those were the fellowship years when roles were reversed and I became the hunter, and guided for both him and his friends. This was a very special time of accepting the responsibility of caring for both the people and the lake that we all loved. The guiding jobs allowed me a summer and holiday income. During my college years, I guided sportsmen who stayed at the small motel that Chester built for his retirement.

As years passed, Chester finally quit hunting. The last time he went out was the winter of 1960. I had just married and started my own business. Chester and I went out for opening day to the old blind and spent most of the morning sharing stories and remembering.

Before he went in at the end of the day, he worked that last bunch of mallards in front of the blind and neatly dropped a big greenhead as he had so many times before. As he thanked me for the hunt that day, he gave me his old shell box, call and gun. After that time, he would just listen to stories about current conditions and hunts that I went on without him. He always wound up our visits with one of our old stories that meant so much to us. They all started with, "Do you remember the time...?"

I hope all of you have in your life an older hunting friend like Chester to enjoy and remember on those cold sunrises when the north wind blows. By the way, Chester was not only my "older duck hunter," he was my Dad.

Dad lived in our home for his last year and what a great experience it was for the whole family. He passed away before the hunting season in 1979 after enjoying a great day visiting and watching football games.

The greatest thing that Dad did for each of my family was the life lessons and the blessings he gave each of us. He never missed the opportunity to thank us for the things we did for him and bless us for who we are. He was special.

FOSTER STRADER

Foster came into my life when I was about ten years old. He was my next door neighbor at the lake and my friend, Jerry's, dad. When we came to the lake on weekends and after I would do my "coming to the lake chores" (grass cutting, camp and boat cleanup), I would head for the Strader house. Jerry's mom, Onis, always had a snack handy and Foster had an update on the lake happenings.

Foster was a wonderful man who lived a good, simple life doing what he wanted to do the best he knew how. He never drove a car, was a local World War II hero, a great duck caller, pistol and shotgun shot, fisherman, father, husband and guide.

He taught by example great truths such as love and help your neighbor, always do your best, don't quit, enjoy the little things in life, be prepared.

FOSTER STRADER

When Russell asked me to write something about my husband, Foster Strader, I found it rather hard to do. I have many memories, of course, but I have to try to select the things that people who will read this book would find most interesting.

Foster lived up on the north end of Reelfoot from the time he was a young boy of fifteen or sixteen. He came to live with his grandparents and uncle. The uncle was only one year older than Foster and they became almost like brothers. Hubert Woods knew the lake as few people did and he taught Foster how to catch the big bass, crappie, bream and of course, how to bring down the ducks during duck season. Foster loved every minute of it and he learned fast.

He loved the lake, his home and family and he only left it twice. Once he and three more men decided to go to Michigan and get jobs. They had relatives up there and they said that jobs were plentiful and the pay good. So, off they went to seek their fortune. We wives stayed home, keeping the home fires burning and taking care of the children.

Two of the men came back home in less than two weeks but Foster and one more stayed on for two months. Foster had a good job. His boss liked him and urged him to stay but Foster had had enough of the Big City and he came home. Later he said he wouldn't live in Detroit, Michigan if they gave him Cadillac Square. He meant it too.

He left the lake one more time. He received a letter from Uncle Sam with the famous word "Greetings," which notified him when and where he was to report to join the Army. It was no surprise. World War II had been going on a long time and just about every man had to go. Married, single, with children - everyone. Of course, some men asked for and got a deferment. But those who did this, unless they had a really legitimate reason, were looked on with much scorn. Foster never even thought of trying for a deferment. He had three brothers who went - Paul, Charles and V. A. He also had many cousins and a brother-in-law in service so he kissed us goodbye and joined the Army.

He was shipped to Camp Robinson near Little Rock, Arkansas. He was placed in the infantry and his basic training was there. It was summertime and very hot. He said their chiggers were every bit as big as the Reelfoot ones - maybe bigger. He finished his training, came home on furlough, then was sent to California where he embarked for Japan. He was very lucky. When their ship was about half way there, the war ended. They went on, of course, and were stationed at Tokyo for eleven months. He found out later that the ship he went over on brought back his brother, Charles. After Foster's tour of duty ended, he came home to the lake and he never left again.

We built a house which I still live in and he went to work guiding and net fishing while I stayed home with our two children, Jerry and Nancy.

My father and mother, George and Ora Gray owned Gray's Camp (a fishing and hunting camp) and my sister Eunice Fox helped them run it. Eunice's husband died about a year or two after returning from the war.

We thought life would go on this way forever, I guess. But in 1955 on December 6th, we received the worst message a parent can get. Our son, Jerry, not quite eighteen and a senior in high school, had died in a car crash. This was a devastating blow to all of us - one you just never quite get over. He and Russell, the author of this book, were good buddies - hunting together and just being boys. Russell still talks to me about Jerry. He has some good memories that we both share.

Jerry's death changed us a lot. I don't think any of us were ever quite the same after that. Foster had great difficulty dealing with the death of our only son, as did we all, my parents, sister and of course Jerry's eleven year old sister, Nancy. But with much help from God, family and friends, we survived.

A few years later, my dad passed away and exactly one year and four months later we were totally shocked and stunned when Foster died of a heart attack. Only fifty-two and apparently very healthy, he passed away in his boat right in front of our house. Nancy was away at Southwestern College in Memphis. We had talked to her on Sunday night. On Monday aft, I had to go to Memphis and tell her, her beloved daddy was dead. It was a terrible blow to all of us.

Today, Nancy lives in Mt. Juliet, Tennessee - happily married with her own private school that she has run for eighteen years. She has a son, Bobby, now twenty-nine and a daughter, Lee, twenty-five. Nancy's husband is an engineer. Nancy often talks of her "Daddy." He is her hero and I am glad. He was indeed "her Superman," and well he deserves to be. A kind and loving man, a gentle man, a man of great integrity. We will not and can not ever forget how bigger than life "Daddy Foster" was. He was truly a good person and a great guide.

Back in the days of World War II, the leader of our country and our allies were referred to as "the big four." President Roosevelt was, of course, our very famous leader, Churchill was England's Prime Minister, DeGaulle, the leader of France and Stalin, the Russian leader.

At Gray's Camp on upper Blue Basin, Reelfoot Lake, we teasingly referred to some of the guides as the "Big Four" as well. This was because they were the four guides most often called for when people were planning a fishing or hunting trip. I won't call the other names but Foster was one of the "Big Four." When a person has gone hunting or fishing with a certain guide, they get accustomed to him and they always want him. If he is already engaged with someone else, the person is almost always unhappy and disappointed. I once heard one man refer to his guide for the day as "just a boat-riding guide." I didn't say anything but I happened to know he was one of the best guides on the lake. The only problem - he wasn't who the man was used to.

Foster, through the years guided many people, rich, poor, some famous and some just average people. He treated them all the same. But, of course, he had his favorite people. He was especially fond of the Blackjack Club and the Blue Wing Club members. He'd guided them for years and he felt close to them and they felt the same by him. I re-read some of his letters from Japan recently and in them he was telling me how sad it made him feel to hear that Mr. Clay Lewis (a member of the Blackjack Club) had died. They indeed, became very close - almost like family and we grieved when we would hear of a death of one of them and it was the same with them.

When Foster died very suddenly of a heart attack one beautiful May morning in 1964, I received so many letters, telegrams and phone calls. A few of the club members were here and came to see us. The florist in Tiptonville said, "You all must have many friends in Clarksville, I've received so many calls for flowers." Yes we did have many friends in Clarksville, indeed, in a number of states who thought a lot of their big guide.

So, what was so special about this big guide whom people felt so deeply about? He was big - a little over six feet tall - broad shouldered with the muscles and strength of an outdoor man. He had arms like the picture on the Arm and Hammer baking soda box - he really did - not from lifting weights, but from rowing Reelfoot boats; blue eyes, sandy hair and of course, sun tanned from the summer sun. He smoked a pipe and he smiled often but never talked much.

When the other guides would sit around the store at Gray's Camp, they'd talk about fishing, hunting and the usual tales of big fish they'd caught or lost or the ducks they'd shot or missed on Reelfoot. Foster rarely said anything but they all liked him. They knew if he did say something it would be the truth. He didn't tell tall tales.

Last summer I came home one day to find a Texas van in my yard. A man got out and came toward me. He put out his hand and said, "You may not remember me." I admitted that I did not. He replied, "I am Lloyd Easterling, Jr." Of course I remembered him then. I had not seen Lloyd since he was thirteen years old. But he and his brother, Warren, used to come to the Blue Wing Club with their dad. Mr. Easterling started bringing Lloyd when he was two years old and when Warren came along, Mr. Easterling brought him as well. Foster guided them so I knew them well.

I invited Lloyd and his wife in and we had a nice visit chatting about the old days. I was amazed at how much Lloyd remembered about Foster. He recalled the kind of hunting clothes Foster wore and the boots - big boots folded over at the knee. The guides called them gum boots and they wore them everyday. They did not have the insulated clothes the hunters wear now, but they wore long under-wear, sweat shirts, wool shirts, two pair of socks (one pair wool) and heavy, brown, stiff, water repellant duck back pants. Lloyd said "Foster was my hero, I wanted to be just like him when I grew up."

Russell says the same thing. I am constantly amazed how many memories of Foster that Russell has. Like Lloyd, he remembers the clothes, the boat, even his cap and Russell tells me of things I didn't know about crossing the frozen lake on a boat with runners. I, of course, saw Foster going across the lake using the runners but Russell had experiences with Foster that I didn't know.

Our daughter, Nancy, has many memories of her dad. After Jerry's death she recalls that she wanted to go rabbit hunting with her dad. I think she was trying to take away the emptiness that Foster felt. He took her out that day - it was cold - almost zero. After a while, she grew so tired and cold. She said, "Daddy, I don't think I can walk any farther." He picked her up, put her on his back and carried her a long way - and she was eleven years old. She said, "I don't see how he did it."

Some years later she was in college. He talked to me and asked me if I cared if he took her out duck hunting when she came home at Christmas. To do this, we had to get out Jerry's gun, have the stock repaired and let her use it. I told him I didn't care. Russell, for his love of Jerry and Foster, repaired the gun and brought it back to Foster. Later, Foster caressed the gun and said softly, "Poor little fellow, he came over to my duck blind just two or three days before he got killed. His gun had hung up and he asked me to fix it." Foster's memories were very strong that day and so were mine.

Later he did take Nancy hunting. It wasn't a very successful hunt. She shot at some coots and hit them. They began to flutter and she threw down the gun and began to cry. She never went hunting again. He talked to me several times about it. He said, "I didn't realize that little old thing was so tender hearted." I laughed and replied, "Some duck hunter you've got."

Many times after Jerry died, when Foster wasn't working, he would go over to his duck blind and stay all day. It would be so cold, close to zero, windy, maybe spitting snow. He would never even fire his gun. I'd ask why he'd go out in the cold and not even shoot his gun. He would say, "I just like to work them and see them coming in. They are so pretty." I think too, he felt closer to Jerry out there.

Foster has been gone a long time now. He sleeps beside our son, my dad, mom and my sister Eunice. I hope our beloved son, other loved ones and old friends were there to greet Foster when he crossed the great divide.

Onice Gray Strader

Foster Strader

DORTCH OLDHAM

I met Dortch when I was a student at the University of Tennessee at Martin. He was a territorial sales manager of Southwestern Company in Nashville, Tennessee. He gave me my first real or formal job (other than working for the family business), selling books door to door in the summer. His leadership and commitment to a job he loved allowed me the opportunity to continue my education and learn a life's profession in sales.

Dortch's personal interest in me changed the way I thought about a lot of things. He taught that you got out of any task what you put into it. If you associated with success and successful people, you would be successful. He was the first person to talk to me about the Bible principle of tithing (giving back 10% to the Lord). What a great blessing this discipline has been. I will always be appreciative that he took the time and entrusted these things to me and is still so special. I spent the day with him and his wife, Sis, at Tom and Sherry Hendrix's great furniture store, Henco, last year. It was a great time for all of us.

Tom Hendrix, Dortch Oldmam and me.

"Chubby" Andrews with Bo-Whoop in Lost Pond

"Chubby" and Marje Andrews

DR. W. F. "CHUBBY" ANDREWS

Chub came into my life in 1981 on a Reelfoot Lake duck hunt. He is the most unique and special person I ever met, he has traveled the world over. He is a great surgeon, Christian missionary, hard hunter, fisherman, taxidermist and spends each day seeing how many things he can do from dawn till dark. Enjoying each day and the bounty of nature, he has a great love of life and a thankfulness for the source of that life.

He has been God's man for my life and has done more to give an example of God's love for me than anyone. What a special privilege and joy his time with me has been. We have traveled the country near and far as hunting, fishing and worship companions.

When I first met Chub I was a tired and burned out Christian deacon. I had been in a negative situation with big church politics and I had lost my joy and sense of direction as a responsible Christian leader.

Through Chubby's prayers and council, our Lord redirected Donna and me into youth work and the Centrifuge program. What a great time of renewed blessing and growth.

Then we were "Lord directed" in late 1992, to our little church home in Samburg where we now serve in an area left vacant by the passing of a special friend, Harvell Denton. These have been some of our best times.

Now, Chub and his wife, Marje, are enjoying some great times traveling the country, seeing old friends in new places and still making great memories.

Harold R. Caldwell and HRC Champion Tracer of Gum Point

HAROLD R. CALDWELL

My special son, Harold, left this world February 14, 2003 on Valentine's Day for a new home with old friends, family and his Lord. He is in a wonderful place where he got a new body and some rewards for things he had done during his earthly journey. He is my special mentor for the things he taught me with his life.

He always looked forward to each new day and he would always try to get the best out of each situation with the help of his helpers and family. He believed that persistence was the greatest of all keys to success. He would work toward the goal, whatever it was, with all he could be and enlisted all the help and support available to the situation.

He had the gift of influence, people loved and honored him. Several of his support staff became Christians while helping him live his earthly life. One of the many things he gave me was his love for others. He taught me the meaning of caring and putting others first, a tough lesson for me, but another of the Christian gifts that our Lord gives.

He had a great love for his church family and the worship experiences shared with them. He helped start a college scholarship program for church members and used his resources to help fund it. He was also instrumental in helping establish two handicap hunting areas on Reelfoot Lake, and used his resources to fund the blinds and wells for the areas. Both blinds have blessed hundreds of disadvantaged hunters and their supporters with hunting opportunities which could not have been realized otherwise.

QUOTES

For God so loved the world that he gave his one and only son that whoever believes in him shall not perish but have eternal life.
The Bible - John 3-16

The view from a duck blind looking over a spread of decoys into a rising sun is like looking straight into the eyes of God.
Bob Hubbs

Memory now takes me back more than fifty years to the Illinois River and the happiest days of my life, and I seem to see the old campgrounds, bluffs, points of timber, bends of the river and shooting grounds, just as I saw them in the long, long ago.
Fred Kimble

As long as there is a duck, there will be duck call makers trying to carry on a more intelligent conversation.
Howard Harlan

We are in a world of beauty but how few of us open our eyes to see it? What a different world this would be if our eyes and ears were trained to see and hear that we are heirs of wonderful treasures from past and present.
Lexie Leonard

Always consider advise given, by what the giver has to gain that gives it.
Chester Caldwell

It was a late winter's afternoon and in all my seventy eight years, I've never seen the lake as it was that day. We walked along the lake. All was a soft grey - a mist or light fog hovered over the whole landscape and sky. It was ethereal, mystical! We both commented on the beauty of our beloved lake. No one was in sight.
Katherine Dietzel Cox

After my father got the corn laid by and the wheat thrashed he would always take the family to Reelfoot Lake on a camping trip to Shaw's Park. Those days you did not have cars or trucks; everything was horse, buggy, surreys and wagon.
Ed Dietzel

About Dortch Oldham: He communicates his faith in you. When you are in trouble he tells you to go back out and turn things around. His faith in you turns out to be the strongest motivation you could have for trying again.
Bill Cook

After you reach sixty five you are capable of many challenges because you have more tools in your "tool chest" than ever before.
Tom Hendrix

The true mark of a man is to stand firm in the face of danger.
Pat Childress

On those rare late autumn days when the air is crisp and I find myself standing on the edge of a field at the end of the day, I am awe struck by the beauty and the power of the Almighty.
Larry Hickerson

You tell me how many you killed and I'll tell you if you had a good hunt.
Billy Wayne Orr

You have to put some shot in the air before anything falls.
Buddy Sedberry

If these happy memories of days afield and joyous play, of deep and abiding friendships, can awaken in your heart and mind a renewed sense of love and loyalty to our hunting heritage and a feeling of gratefulness for what the beauty and the inspiration of nature have meant to you; then time and effort spent on writing this book has served a wonderful purpose.
Wayne Capatooth

Miles and memories are best made with dear friends and family.
Patrick Pitt

A mind, like a home, is furnished by its owner, so if one's life is cold and bare he can blame none but himself. You have a chance to select from some pretty elegant furnishings. Louis L'Amour

I am ever grateful for friendships for they are the greatest assets a man can have.
Spence Dupree

Life is not about always getting to do things you like to do, but learning to like what you have to do.
Chester Caldwell

Bloom where you are planted, make a decision that you're going to make the most of the situation. Happiness is a choice.
Joel Osteen

Ask and it shall be given you, seek and you shall find, knock and it will be opened to you.
The Bible - Matthew 7-7

The most important thing in life is to have a ticket for the Heavenly Train when it pulls out.
"Cotton" Ivy

You must lead by example. Never ask someone to do something you wouldn't do or haven't done yourself. While leading you should be beyond reproach and always set a good example for others to follow.
Buddy Makin

Failing to prepare is preparing to fail.
John Wooden

The meeting before the meeting is the one that counts.
Caleb L. Davis III

If you treat everyone the same, then you treat no one special.
Russell Caldwell

Right beliefs dictate right behavior.
Bob Latta

Service to others due to love. This is the purpose of a Christian life.
Donna Caldwell

There are no ifs in the sovereign plan of God.
Ken Whitten

The water is so still
It looks like a mirror if you will
Or a picture postcard of some place off afar
But then who takes time to see the beauty where we are?
Roger Badger

I love to tell the old stories.
Harbert Alexander

Cypress and Ice.

No one on their death bed has ever said, "I wish I had spent more time on my business!"
Carl Kirkland

If all the "ifs" and "buts" were candies and nuts, then the world would be full of riches.
Alan Dement

Some people know the cost of everything but know the value of nothing.
Ken Whitten

Seeing the road is different from walking the road.
Luke Burnett

A man of word and not of deeds is like a garden full of weeds.
Charles Crowell

Once you get Reelfoot Lake in your blood you will always come back.
Cris Badger

I'm always sleepy on opening day because I'm awake all night the night before.
Sammy Algee

The situation is . . .
Harold Caldwell

A memory is a memory only as long as someone remembers it, but when you write it down it remains a memory forever.
Evelyn Norris

Do not be envious of someone else's successes if you are not willing to do what they had to do to get it.
Pam Prather

A lot of things are better remembered than experienced.
Charles Berry

You get everything in life you want if you help enough other people get what they want.
Zig Zigler and Rob Caldwell

O Lord at daybreak you will hear my voice and I will wait expectantly for your answer.
Marje Andrews

Hunting skill is fooling the birds.
Mike Fraley

If it's worth doing it's worth doing right, so follow the directions.
Melba Jo Childress

STORIES
POEMS
ESSAYS

THE LETTER

DONNA CALDWELL
1453 Lake Drive
Hornbeak, TN 38232-3235

Phone: 731-538-2588
Fax: 731-538-2888
e-mail: clc@cebridge.net

April 30, 2003

Dear BMH Classmates,

While cleaning off my desk (a miraculous happening in it-self) I came across a letter from one "Shirley Dill Pepper" dated November 20, 1999. Has it really been that long since our class reunion? A lifetime in some ways. I wish to thank each of you for allowing me to relate to you at the time of the reunion, some of the happenings of my life in the sorrows of my son's illness. It was a first in acknowledging publicly that indeed my son had an illness that would cause his death and not in the distant future.

The Lord is to be praised mightily for His precious care of us. It has been almost four years now since the reunion and He has given my family many wonderful memories and definitely carried us along the way. Easter Sunday, March 31, 2002 as we were getting him dressed for church, Harold took a giant step toward going home to his heavenly father. My husband Russell's quick work and a quick response from church family providing oxygen allowed Harold to endure until an ambulance arrived. Upon arrival at the emergency room we were told that if he had been five minutes longer getting to the hospital all systems would have shut down. After a three day stay in the hospital stabilizing, we returned home to cope with oxygen therapy.

For a few months prior to this occasion Harold was limited to being out of bed only long enough for his daily shower (via hoyer lift and wheel chair) and going to church on Sunday mornings for an hour, out to a quick lunch and back to bed. He soon was insisting on going back to church. We took him to the church service only and then straight home. Even this was very tiring for him. The church family, recognizing that he might not be able to attend much longer, designated Sunday May 5, 2002 as Harold Caldwell Appreciation Day. During that Sunday morning service he was presented a plaque of appreciation from the church for his inspiration to them and his dedication to funding the scholarship program which we have in our church. The presentation was made by the young people who had and were still benefiting from the program. After the church services, as Baptist so often do, we had dinner at the church.

He missed a few Sundays out of the next five months and made a big effort to attend October 20, 2002 which was Homecoming Sunday. That was his last time out of the house. His brother and a friend put a wildlife Christmas tree up in his room before Thanksgiving and each week would come bearing a gift for him to open and watch television with him. We had frequent family gatherings including many children who gathered around him, watching TV and movies with him. We ate many of our meals in the room with him. He loved the company. This was also a very traumatic time. He had about two weeks of oxygen equipment gradually becoming dysfunctional without our realizing that was the problem. It was agonizing for him and for us. Correcting the problem made life easier for him, but he did not regain any ground lost.

The new year found all of us weary and wondering who would out last whom. I asked God if Harold was to outlast us and have to face life lying there unable to move anything and be without the support of either of us. Was this what He intended for my husband and me for the rest of our lives, caring for Harold? Did He not have any other work planned for us by which He could be glorified? I told Him we were willing to continue as we were with Harold for the rest of our lives if that was His will, but please Lord don't let him agonize for breath again. I don't think I could stand it. If it be your will Lord let him go in his sleep quietly. Lord, how can I face losing him? How will I react? How can I bear the pain? David was able to rejoice after his son died. Is it possible Lord that I could rejoice then too?

About three weeks later, February 14, 2003, yes, on Valentine's Day, I walked into Harold's room at 6:10 am to check on him and he was taking his last breath, quietly, in his sleep. Yes, the time of visitation and the next day of funeral were a time of celebration. The Lord had given both my husband and me David's joy. We have wonderful days of joyous remembrance and then again we have days like today when the remembering is with great fondness but with tears. Tears of sadness for his trials, but of gladness for the ministry he was to others. Tears from missing him. Healing tears. There haven't been many, but they are beginning to come more freely. He was always so easy to love. We adapted our lives to him as he became walker and wheelchair bound. We adapted to living a great part of our lives in his room as he became bedfast. We adapted to having a helper in our home around the clock. Never alone. One of the helpers was with us for three days straight every three days for six years. My now five year old granddaughter thought he was my son too. She loves him like an uncle and we do feel like he is a part of the family. God provided us with such a myriad of workers on the other half of that shift. That could be a book in itself.

Life marches on and yes God is using us in many ways. Russell has found a gift he never dreamed of having. The gift of service. (He already had more than most of us see in ourselves.) In his heart he still needs to take Harold riding to check out the animals and crops in the refuge. Finding an ailing friend who needs time and attention, off they go. There are those who have problems similar to some Harold had and we have been able to advise them and their families on good and proven ways to meet their needs. We are more aware of the needs of others now and have a greater boldness in trying to help meet those needs. We see opportunities to serve God by ministering to His children in different ways every day. Our grandchildren have benefited from Harold's illness by being more accepting and comfortable with anyone who has to deal with life in a way different from the average person. We are glad that He is ours and we are His. Harold would have been 33, July 19th of this year.

May God bless and keep each of you and your families.

In His Love,

Donna Hauser Caldwell

P.S. We are expecting a new grandson about the 19th of June.

Nash Buckingham

Photograph courtesy of Dr. "Chubby" Andrews

I Wish . . .

I wish…all alone in the shack tonight
While the clock ticktocks, and the fire glows bright,
And a wind that howls through treetops tall
Is the voice of a brusque old friend…that's all.
I wish…where shadows and rafters reach,
There are pictures, too, with a story each,
Of men, and dogs, and days astray . . .
In their Lifelong Valley called Come-What May.
So I close my book and shut my eyes,
And sigh to myself - "Gosh, how Time flys."
Was it yesterday, from this dear old camp,
That I hit the trail, so eager to tramp
Hand in hand with my comrade - Youth -
With its job in hardship, and trust in Truth?
With never a care save fun of the thing,
Nor a hang for footing next day might bring?
Up ere dawn, afield with the sun,
Plodding on home when the light was done,
Come snow and ice, come rain or shine,
Just me and my gun and Daddy o'Mine.
I wish . . . but the years have asked their pay,
Hair that was brown is streaked with gray.
But urge of Youth still lingers strong,
While there's life to fun, I'll hustle on.
I wish…by glory of bygone joys,
By that boundless Open that beckons all boys -
That their days may be long, and the winding call
Of some hunter's horn - will reach them all.
And I pray…by the soul of a Lad-at-War,
Keep your eyes front, Jim-Boy, where'er you are-
May God bring you home…warm your whole life through
-
And your Pals in Camp - be like those I knew.

Nash Buckingham

It's been years since Reelfoot Lake
held this number of ducks.
Photograph courtesy of Jim Johnson

POLAR ROLLER

Cold fronts almost always bring the ducks!! The most enthusiasm I've ever seen is a duck hunter watching the Weather Channel with a cold front coming. He can barely sleep with the anticipation of a "migration" on it's way!

I've seen many cold fronts in my 30 years of duck hunting. One that sticks out in my mind was in December 1995. Dad and I along with some of our huntin' buddies came in off the lake from hunting and went straight to the TV and turned to the Weather Channel as we did many days to see if there was a cold front on the horizon promising a migration of new birds to our area. "New Ducks" are always easier to work because they haven't seen your decoy spread day after day. The area is new, your hunting spot is new to the ducks, and the big bunches ball up from the skies and fall down into your decoys. This particular cold front was exciting because the Weather Channel predicted it a week in advance and named it the "Polar Roller". We went hunting each morning more excited than the day before - laughing and joking about the "Polar Roller" and how we were going to tear them up when it got here.

To our surprise about four days before the predicted cold front, the ducks started coming. We started seeing the skies fill up with high bunches of every kind of duck. BIG bunches! Flying HIGH! We would "high ball' and here they would come. We killed a limit of ducks all four days in front of the "Polar Roller" and each day we saw more ducks and killed our limits quicker. The shooting on Reelfoot Lake was so much and so often that it sounded like a war (and we felt like we were winning). Each day we were more excited than the day before reminding each other that if this is good, it will only get better when the "Polar Roller" gets here!! We laughed, cut up and took lots of pictures of our daily kill. Each day we took more hunters so we could bag more birds. The night before the fifth day we could not sleep for the excitement of how good tomorrow was going to be. We relished our victories of the four days leading up to the "Polar Roller" and kept saying each day how good the migration is going to be when it gets here. How many ducks will we see and bag on the "Polar Roller" day? We had just been experiencing days with ducks bagged in the 40's and 50's. Just how good was the big day going to be?

Well, the next morning, the day of the "Polar Roller" it was so cold that on the boat ride out to the blind any man that wasn't driving a boat was sitting with his back towards the front of the boat dodging that north wind. It was so cold that every wave that splashed on the boat sent a spray onto the hunters that froze to our hunting coats. By the time we reached Lost Pond, our open water blind on Reelfoot Lake, we were all frozen stiff. We had to break the ice off our coats to move our arms. We got into the blind and Dad began telling us of a day, November 11, 1940, when a storm called Armistice came and the wind was so high and the temperature so cold that hunters died, and some, hunting on islands, chopped up their boats and burned them for fire wood to keep warm. That was not a very comforting story to us as we were already cold as heck. As daylight broke we stayed down and held our calls and guns, one in each hand. We were staying down to not spook the first flight of mallards and we were still dodging that extremely cold north wind blowing between 25 and 30 miles an hour placing the wind chill well below zero. As sunrise broke, much to our surprise the sky was empty. There were no sounds in the distance of other hunters shooting or calling for that matter. The war was over! The ducks came ahead of the front this time and I can't say as I blame them because it was about the coldest day I ever remember hunting. Our cokes froze in the can and our Snickers were frozen so hard that you couldn't bite into them. We wound up getting one Jack Attack (that is a flock of Black Jacks/

Ring-necks flying so fast that you feel as if you are being attacked) and we were so stoved up from the cold that out of a blind full of capable shooters we only knocked down two. . I couldn't believe that after all that anticipation and four of the best days of waterfowling I ever experienced, it ended on two ducks after we killed almost 200 the four days leading up to the "Polar Roller".

Dad always told me, "Learn from the past and you will be better prepared for your future." I believe the lesson to be learned from the "Polar Roller" is don't rush through the good days waiting for your best. Because one day you will wake up and realize the war is over. The fun is done. And you rushed your way through the good days always expecting it to get better. Find something to enjoy in each day. Love the Lord. Cherish your wife. Respect your parents. Appreciate the privilege of being on this earth for a short period of time hunting, fishing and preserving the sport for others to enjoy!

Robert E. Caldwell

Photograph courtesy of Jim Johnson

THE RIVER

There's a fever raging,
    in the hearts of some,
How long it lasts I do not know
    nor when it first begun.

I only know I'm different
    from lots of other men,
Where they fear to travel
    I've already been.

The game I play is tough at best
    The River has its terms,
Yet the love to hunt the mighty Miss
    within my heart still burns.

There are other places one could hunt
    easier to be sure,
Yet ole Miss is different,
    she casts a magic lure.

Here's a truth that some folk know
    my friends who know me well,
the River has me in its grasp
    I'm caught within her spell.

And when I'm old and all worn out
    and the River's just too much,
I'll quit a little earlier
    And make it home for lunch.

The Mississippi River
    holds me with its lore,
I know I'll hunt the River
    until I hunt no more.

Bob Anderson

From left to right:
Dr. "Chubby" Andrews - writer and shooter
Tom Makin - Poetry writer and rabbit hunter
Brad Makin - Main son of Buddy
Dave Bethel - Brad's longtime hunting buddy
Sammy Algee - The hardest hunting fellow I know who believes every duck is callable

Le Couier Du Bois
"He Who Runs in the Woods"
or
My Life

Do not cry for me
After I am gone
Just hum me a line
From my favorite song

A man once said
I have seen the promised land
I have walked through it
while many have held my hand

I have sat on top of the mountain
And watched the world awaken
I watched the day lay claim
To what the darkness had taken

I have stood in the shadow
Of a few great men
Someday I hope to see them
And talk with them again

I have watched the wild geese fly
On their journey south
And wonder what they are saying
When that strange cry comes from their mouth

I have watched gray squirrels
Laying in their winter store
And marveled at the signs of dolphins
Playing along the Gulf Shore

I have watched the deer
Lurking in the shadows of the swamp
I have listened as the coyote announced
The start of his deadly romp

I have spent my life
Walking through fields and woods
Most men I know are envious
And they only wish they could

I have walked the sides of mountains
With a rifle in my hand
And wondered who made the first tracks
Across this formidable land

I have seen huge old trees
As I stumbled through the woods
If they could tell me all they have seen
I know the story would be good

I have walked many miles
Looking at a good hounds tail
And watched him work the coverts
And hear his joyful wail

I have tasted cool sweet water
From a high mountain stream
And filled my lungs with the fresh air
That a summer storm can bring

I have watched the leaves turn
And marvel in God's splendor
And felt the cool breeze on my neck
That promises another hard winter

I have made a few good friends
Who never let me down
And I can think of two grandfathers
Who I wish were still around

When I look at my family
I realize I am truly blessed
Through the years of tears and laughter
They have proven they are the best

Although rare for this day and age
I have lived a life of freedom
A boy who would not grow up
A king walking through his kingdom

I have done about all
That I really wanted to
But there are still some good things left
Come and you can do them too

Thomas Makin
October 7, 2003

Afterthought:

It could be considered a sad state of affairs when one's life
story can be told in a couple of pages. It should be remembered however that quality of life always counts for
more than quantity.

Carpe Diem

Youth

Youth is not a time of life; it is a state of mind; it is not a matter of rosy cheeks, red lips and supple knees; it is a matter of the will, a quality of the imagination, a vigor of the emotions; it is the freshness of the deep springs of life.

Youth means a temperamental predominance of courage over timidity, of the appetite for adventure over the love of ease. This often exists in a man of sixty more than a boy of twenty. Nobody grows old merely by a number of years. We grow old by deserting our ideals.

Years may wrinkle the skin, but to give up enthusiasm wrinkles the soul. Worry, fear, self-distrust bows the heart and turns the spirit back to dust.

Whether sixty or sixteen, there is in every human being's heart the lure of wonder, the unfailing child-like appetite of what's next, and the joy of the game of living. In the center of your heart and my heart there is a wireless station; so long as it receives messages of beauty, hope, cheer, courage and power from men and from the Infinite, so long are you young.

When the aerials are down, and your spirit is covered with snows of cynicism and the ice of pessimism, then you are grown old, even at twenty, but as long as your aerials are up, to catch the waves of optimism, there is hope you may die young at eighty.

Samuel Ullman

DOWN AT PAUL AND MARY KATHERINE'S PLACE

As I approach the setting sun and the
end of Life's day,
I think of beloved comrades afield
I have known along the way.
The happy times we have shared in the
battle of come what may……
My heart goes out to them and I am lead
to pray
That they may experience too, the love of
God, His wondrous Grace.
And have the joy of knowing and
Sharing the wonderful love and
Friendship like I have had,
Down at Paul and Mary Katherine's Place.

William F. Andrews

SHAPING YOUR LIFE

The way you see your life shapes your life. The best way to understand other people is to ask them "How do you see your life?" The image that comes to mind is their "life metaphor." It is the view of life they hold consciously or unconsciously in their mind. It is their description of how life works and what they expect from it. People often express their life metaphor through clothes, jewelry, cars, hair styles, bumper stickers even tattoos.

Your unspoken metaphor determines your expectations, your values, your relationships, your goals, and your priorities. To fulfill the purposes God made you for you will have to challenge conventional wisdom and replace it with biblical metaphores of life. The Bible says "Do not conform yourselves to the standards of this world, but let God transform inward by a complete change of your mind." Then you will be able to know the will of God. The Bible offers three metaphores that teach God's view of life. Life is: a test, a trust, and a temporary assignment.

God says "They are my own people and I created them to bring me glory." Living for God's glory should be the supreme goal of our lives. God is inviting us to enjoy him. He wants our worship to be motivated by love, thanksgiving and delight, not duty. God is most glorified in us when we are most satisfied in Him. Worship is a lifestyle of enjoying God, loving Him and giving ourselves to be used for his purpose. When you use your life for God's glory everything you do can become an act of worship. God gave you a new life and a new nature when you accepted his son as your savior. My new life was that I knew that I was now accepted by God as God's child with much love.

Donna H. Caldwell

HUNTING TALES

LIFE OF A GLODO DUCK CALL

My first experience in life was of the touch of my maker's hands. Victor Glodo, with the quick hands of a master craftsman, finished my barrel by scraping me smooth with a piece of broken glass, then checkering my surface with his Barlow pocket knife. He bored a hole in my barrel with an old hand brace and bit; then carefully finished my surface with sandpaper, oil and varnish.

Many hours were spent getting my insert and tone channel just right. Each day, after gunning the lake, helping dress the day's kill, and loading the old brass hulls for another day, my maker would spend some time sanding my brass reed to the proper thickness. He would comment again to his wife, Veda, about the difficulty in getting the brass from the old whiskey still just right. Soon my wedge block was being worked down and the final fitting was taking place with the insert, reed and block. At last my maker, Glodo, had me together for the first blowing. It surely was exciting for me! He tied a loop in a piece of net line, then tied the other end around me and carefully placed me with a brother call in the old shell box he used.

My first day with Victor out on the lake was special for both of us. After using his regular call for the first part of the morning, he took me out for a try. On my first high ball, that big bunch caved in and sailed into our wooden blocks. It was my first taste of the excitement of the birds, calling and gunning as a total experience. It surely was fine! Victor turned me over in his rough waterman's hand and said, "You surely have a real ring; we're going to have a time today." The next bunch came over Grassy Bend from the north and my maker and I got on them in earnest. After a ringing high ball and a couple of short hail calls they swung around the hole. I put a quarter turn on and teased them with a few quacks and clucks, but they still weren't ready for the skillet shoot and they drifted off again. Victor said to get on them hard, and he blew the old paralyzer lay-down call at them. With that lick, the old lead greenhead snapped around for the finish. My master dropped me to his chest and I hung there and watched him raise his old 97 Winchester...and four beautiful mallards stayed behind. We tallied 150 mallards that day and shot clean out of shells. Man, it was great!

We lived on Starve Island in Reelfoot Lake in those years. Each fall Victor would get things ready for the fall season; painting decoys, loading shells, buying supplies for winter, but always with an eye turned north for the beginning of the flight. There were several of us "calls" in the old shell box and each year some of the other market hunters in the area would talk Victor out of some of us, but I was his favorite and I got to spend most of my time in his coat pocket on my tarred string. I learned to do all the calls with such a mellow tone that I was hard to resist, and we had the largest kills of all the locals.

Then things changed. Victor became ill and had to leave the Island and move to Samburg. He found a hollow in the hills outside of town and built us a small house there. Our hunts were fewer each season and one fall one of the Johnson brothers (who had gotten one of my shell-box mates the year before) came by with his brother and got Victor to part with me.

My life after Victor was different; the birds were fewer in number, the government set seasons and limits were enforced. The Johnsons used their Glodo calls well, but it was different. The master's touch was lacking. The Johnsons had some trouble; my shell-box mate was traded to Bill Nation and I was passed on to family member, Babe Johnson, one of Union City's shooting champions.

Babe was a Remington Arms exhibition shooter in the late 1930 and 1940 period. He loved to shoot skeet, and the story was told that in the war years Remington gave him only a box of shells per day. During that time, he never missed a single target -- quite a record! In the late 1940's Babe owned M & W Hardware Store in Union City, which became the hang-out for local hunters and target shooters. He was well known as a fine duck shot and hunted often with the Reelfoot guides.

This Johnson considered me a keepsake, so I commenced my life in a cigar box. I don't know how many years I spent there, but one day the box was opened by Mrs. Johnson and I was shown to a collector who wanted to take me to meet a call collector from Nashville for an opinion about my authenticity. A meeting was scheduled. The Nashville collector looked me over carefully -- even counted the lines in my checkering patterns, stating that they were the same pattern as my old shell-box mate's who now resided in the Johnny Marsh collection in Nashville.

My new owner will never blow me at the northern birds I was designed to lure, but he will display me with pride as one of the best of my kind, honoring Victor Glodo, my maker.

Photography by Jim Johnson

THE DAY THE WORLD TURNED TO DUCKS

Many of you will remember this day as I describe it, not from the date (which was January 7, 1976) but from what happened. The morning started as most hunts do except I was hunting by myself and I was getting things ready for some men I had coming in for the next day. When I got on the lake the temperature was in the 40's with a brisk east wind; the trip to the blind was uneventful.

The ducks weren't moving so I left my gun in the case and started rearranging my decoys for the expected wind change. We were still using jugs and I went to Black Jack Pocket to get some extras Steve Russell had given me while he was using Jerry Flippin's blind on the point. When I got back to Lost Pond, I put the jugs with the mass I had behind the blind and got back inside.

It was about 10:00 and I heard a rumbling in the distance that sounded like a train. When I turned to look toward the north across Forked Pond, I could see the storm coming across the lake. I could hear the guns hammering in Grassy Bend and I knew the front was arriving. Looking toward Second Pocket at tree level, there was almost a wall of ducks approaching in big bunches in front of the wind. Before I could get my Winchester out of its case, a bunch of 150 Northern Mallards swarmed into the blocks and the wind arrived seconds later, blowing a gale. Then the bunch flushed and came over the blind. I still wasn't loaded, but it didn't matter because ducks were everywhere! Every blind on Lost Pond had ducks working their spreads and ducks were lighting all over the open water - and no one was there but me. The next bunch came in a wad and I knocked down a couple of greenheads. The temperature was falling fast and it was spitting snow, but the ducks still came. I could hear the guns in the Bend and Rushing Pond, so I knew I had company with this wealth of waterfowl. I took my time with my limit, enjoying the greatest wildlife spectacle I have ever seen.

I finished my ducks shortly after lunch and started to shore amid four-foot waves. The water was freezing on the blocks and stumps and it was bitter cold. On the way in I saw Red Armstrong, and Buddy and Steve Sedberry on their way to their blind and stopped and told them what a picnic they were in for. When I got to camp, I drove to Samburg for lunch and standing outside the restaurant, I could still see the migration pouring in. Guides were coming in with their first bunch of sports hoping to get back out with another group of men. The wind was really hammering and the ice was forming around the shore. The restaurant filled with hard hunters telling tales of how good it was; the excitement was in all of us. Some kneebooters swamped at the mouth of the ditch and some of the Hoggs pulled them out. Johnny Cochran brought his men in from the Isom pit and took them on the lake. Everyone on the lake got a limit of ducks and the same result was had all over West Tennessee -- at Dunlap Bar, Sheeps Ridge, Hatchie, Crockett, Gooch, and Island #8.

That night the lake froze hard and stayed frozen for the rest of the 1976 season, but what a day to end up on!

Photo by Vern Sabin.

TIMES PAST IN SAMBURG

We just arrived, and man, is it cold! Icicles hang from your breath. On the way here the old car broke down and then we had a flat. We sure need a set of tires.

"The War" is still going on, but there are a lot of hunters in for the mallard flight. I saw Spicer come in with his men and they had some of the biggest "Bull Canvasbacks" I have ever seen. Spicer was complaining about his shells. Since the war started, shotgun shells have been hard to get and he has been reloading some old brass hulls he used in the teens. It surely is exciting to watch the guides bring their sports in. They walk the streets with hands full of big ducks and their long-barrel guns tucked under their arms.

It's time to get checked in at the old hotel on the corner. I hope they have heat tonight; it is bitter cold. On the way to the hotel, we stopped by to tell Mr. Bill Nation, our guide, that we had arrived. As usual, we got his grumpy reply, "Well, you're expected." These guides surely have a different attitude about business. They act as if they are doing us a favor by taking us out each day. After all, we pay a fee of fifteen dollars a day per person, plus provide the guide's shells. And Mr. Bill always expects a two-dollar tip.

After checking in and storing our gear, we're now ready for that evening treat of dinner at Boyette's Dining Room. Boyette's is one of the finest restaurants in the country. Man! Smell that country ham, fish and hush puppies. This is the only restaurant in the country that always stuffs a hungry man. The meal is served family style, and there is always plenty.

As we drive back to our hotel, we note that the Lake Club is in rare form, with a big crowd enjoying the evening and avoiding the cold outside. Approaching the hotel, we hear a flock of geese pass overhead, and as always, the hair on the back of my neck lifts at the sound of their haunting cry.

Sleep comes slowly with dreams of big bunches of working ducks for us to enjoy. I always shoot well in my dreams...that sure was a nice double on those climbing mallards.

When morning comes, Mrs. Nation prepares breakfast for us and we get ready for our frigid ride across the lake in Nath Parkinson's covered boat. He is pulling the Reelfoot boats behind his big boat. That wind sure is cold! We have a little trouble in the beginning of the trip. We hit a stump and the motor stalls, but it restarts and the rest of the trip to Horse Island Ditch is uneventful but exciting. Mr. Bill separates from Nath and goes up the ditch to hunt in the hole behind the Gourd.

We are using the north wind blind this morning so the wind is at our backs. There is a thin skim of ice on the blocks, so after putting us in the blind, Mr. Bill starts cleaning up the hole. I don't know why he bothers...ducks are everywhere, and they are working with him in plain view. My friend Jerry is excited. It is his first hunt and the waiting is killing him! Mr. Bill gets back into the blind and lights up his old charcoal stove. The smoke is everywhere. He puts the stove up on the roof of the blind to "catch" better.

Shooting time is fast approaching. We can start shooting thirty minutes before daylight and we start getting ready as Mr. Bill puts the stove back into the blind. The cheeriness of the fire helps fight the cold, but its barely noticed in the building excitement.

As we peer into the cold gray half-light, a bunch of big ducks begin settling into the hole. Mr. Bill grunts into his long barrel call a couple of times and shouts, "GET EM!" I feel Jerry rising beside me as my old Model 12 falls into that familiar pocket between arm and shoulder. My eyes line the barrel on a sailing mallard, I squeeze the trigger, and the duck falls. I pump the hull out and drop another for a clean double. Jerry is so excited! He has his first duck on the water, and Mr. Bill has killed two-for a total of five. The limit this year is ten mallards per day, so we have started off with a bang! As Mr. Bill gets back into the blind from gathering the ducks, he complains about getting his glove wet. The second bunch is a pair of grey ducks that has slipped in behind us and hooked into the wind in front of the blind. Jerry and I make easy shots on these ducks and the one Jerry knocks down is banded. Jerry is so excited at his early success that he misses an easy greenhead that Mr. Bill quacked in.

The day progresses with good food and fellowship, and Mr. Bill tells several of those old stories for which he is famous. After a good lunch fixed over charcoal, we get ready for the afternoon. It has started to spit snow and the new ducks are moving in. Three come in, and three stay! Mr. Bill even comments on our shooting today, and takes a look at my old Winchester.

Our success turns to failure when we don't touch a feather on the next two bunches. Mr. Bill shows us some of that long-range shooting that Reelfoot guides are famous for, killing two high ones out of each from the next two bunches. We wind up our day with the snow really coming down and the "Supper Bunch" coming right at quitting time for us to finish our limits. As we come across the open water, I tell Mr. Bill that Jerry and I have had a great time and that it is the finest day I have ever experienced on waterfowl.

Other hunters have had a big day too. There are over 500 ducks at the pickers behind Bunches' Grocery. What a fine day of good sport and fellowship. It is truly a gift from a kind Heavenly Father.

As we head for Boyette's for another round of that good food, we start thinking about tomorrow.

TOMORROW! The excitement for another day is already building.

Photograph by Vern Sabin

251

Elbert Spicer - Reelfoot guide.
Photograph courtesy of Tennessee Wildlife Resources.

HUNTING WITH OLD MEN

The one thing I learned quickly growing up around hunting and fishing is you always killed more ducks, caught more fish and stayed out of danger when you went with your dad and the old men.

The best thing my dad ever did for me was spend time with me. Some of my best friends have been my dad and the old men that my dad hunted with. Of my young hunting career, my favorite hunting season was the winter of 1979. My dad decided that I was old enough to get up and shoot with him and the old men. Up until that point they occasionally let me shoot first and then every man for himself. I would always pick the candy duck (that is what we call the one that gets the closest). Lots of times I would kill the duck and after that I of course claimed anything else that fell. It was great graduating from sitting on the bench in the back of the blind hiding while they worked the ducks because every time I watched the ducks work while they called, they blamed the ones that didn't work on me. "They are seeing you Rob. You have to be STILL!" (Have you ever heard that one?) I am 37 now and some ducks still don't work when we call them. I never could figure out why they thought the ducks couldn't see them but I was so visible when I was four feet tall and they were over six feet.

It used to blow my mind at that age crossing Reelfoot Lake in the dark on those cold mornings. Dad sat me in front of him facing the back of the boat and I watched every other wave splash on him and freeze to ice as we crossed Lost Pond. One day before we left the bank, he lit the charcoal bucket, which was our heater back then and put it between my legs to keep me warm on the way to the blind. Half way there he hung the wooden Reelfoot Lake boat on a BIG stump and the bucket turned over on my poncho. The hot coals started melting the plastic and falling thru to my clothes. Being the quick thinker he is he grabbed the bailer (a jug cut half into to bail water out of the boat to keep it from swamping) dipped it in the lake and began throwing the water on me. I don't know what was worse . . . being hung on a stump in the middle of Reelfoot Lake in the dark . . . being on fire . . . or having freezing water thrown on your face to put the fire out. When we made it to the blind that morning Dad said to me, "We probably shouldn't tell your Mom about this."

Another fond memory of hunting with the old men was, at lunch time my dad would always go to shore and take a nap after lunch. I would be wound up tighter than a ten day clock, waiting for him to get up so we could go back on the lake and finish our days hunt. On some Saturdays Emery Burden (Mr. B), my Godfather since my middle name is Emery, would let me stay in the blind and continue the hunt with him while Dad went to shore for that dang nap. Well, Emery never cut anybody any slack. When a duck came in whether you were 12 years or 50 years old it was every man for himself. No candy left for the kid. My dad didn't have any old men that he hunted with that weren't crack shots and Mr. B was no exception. I didn't know you could hit something with a shotgun that you couldn't see until one Saturday in the Lost Pond Blind R127 on Reelfoot Lake with Mr. B. I will never forget him calling the shot on three ducks that were in the sun where you couldn't see them, nothing but black dots surrounded by that fire ball sun. Mr. B said those words I'd been waiting on for about 30 seconds as those three ducks circled the blind in shooting range. "GET 'EM." I jumped up with my Remington model 1100 12 gauge shotgun ready to throw 3 at em' and I was blinded by the light. Emery fired three times into the sun and all three mallards splashed on the water. That was 25 years ago and I remember it like it was yesterday! I couldn't wait until my dad got back into the blind so I could tell him how Mr. B hogged me while he was taking a nap. I just knew that he was going to correct him. But when Dad got back and I told my story of how Mr. B hogged me in the sun, my Dad looked down and just grinned.

Another old man that's hunted with us all my life is Dr. William Farr "Chubby" Andrews a general surgeon from Germantown, TN that spent his young life hunting with the renowned sports writer and shotgunner Mr. Nash Buckingham. I used to think that the ducks and geese followed Chubby around because I have never had a bad days hunt with Chubby. There has always been something magical about this old man. He always had a new story to tell about how many ducks he killed, the far off places he hunted them and had the taxidermy to prove it. Chubby has over 1,500 birds mounted in his house on display. (That says a lot about his wonderful wife Marje for putting up with this old man.) The trick I learned from Chubby was in Canada while hunting ducks. In Canada you can hunt ducks for a little while after dark. The trick is can you hit them? Well, Chubby sure can! We were out on a marsh and ducks were everywhere! Canada had no shortage. I would see the shadow of a duck and shoot my gun dry with no bird falling. Chubby was just as deadly as when the sun was up. After shooting a box of shells and not dropping one bird and he had killed his limit, I asked him, "How do you hit these ducks in the dark?" He replied, "Watch the moon and as you see the ducks approach, mount your gun. Follow thru and shoot the duck against the background of the moon before it enters the darkness again." To my surprise, it worked! I killed my limit of ducks in the next half a box of shells. Dr. Chubby mounted a huge gadwall for me that we picked up that night and it is on the wall of my log home at Reelfoot Lake still today.

The winter of 2003, I changed the blind rules for our Lost Pond Blind R127 and started letting my dad shoot first. The ducks are fewer now and you don't get an opportunity to kill as many. We don't take very many people because when the limit is 6 each and you only average killing 10 total, two people can do that legally and get more shooting opportunities. Dad seems to be happy with the role reversal. Yet he sometimes forgets when there is more than one duck to shoot that I am capable of killing my own so he shoots it first and then kills his. At least he does tell me "good shot" and I don't reply since I didn't even fire my gun.

The funny part of this story is that today Chubby is 84, Emery is 80 and my Dad is 67. They really are old men. I referred to them as such all my life and now I am almost the age they were when I considered them to be old when I was just a boy. Everything I know good and bad about hunting waterfowl and hitting birds with a shotgun I learned from these old men. They also taught me lessons in life along the way. Some they told me and some I learned from just paying attention. Remember, some young man is watching your every move and learning by example. Be kind and patient, let the kid have a shot. Set a good example like these Legends did for me.

Robert E. Caldwell

This story was written late on Monday, June 27, 2005 and shared with "Chubby" on the following afternoon. On the afternoon of Wednesday, June 29, 2005, William Farr "Chubby" Andrews quietly left all of us behind and entered a far happier Hunting Ground with his blessed Savior, Jesus the Christ, as his everlasting Guide.

Postscript written by Donna Caldwell

THE CONTEST

This tale was told by Reelfoot hunter and trapshooter John Lykin about an event that took place after live decoys were outlawed in the 1930s, when the duck limit was fifteen per day.

When groups of hunters are sitting around talking, many times the discussion turns to who is the best shot, caller, guide, etc., and such was the case at this happening. The contest started one day after everyone was in off the lake, and enjoying refreshments at Claude Botts' camp in Samburg. The discussion was about who would make up the best team among the top local shots and Reelfoot guides, in a contest to see who could kill a twenty duck limit the quickest on a given day. Twenty dollars per team would be put into the prize money "pot."

Prospects for the match were contacted, teams were formed, and the rules were discussed. It was decided that the winning team would be the first to return to the bank with a twenty-duck bag. Everyone would leave at the same time with 36 decoys in a Reelfoot paddle boat, hunt any-where they wanted, and all ducks had to be taken on the wing.

The teams consisted of:
Jake Gibbs and Jack Hogg
John Lykin and Jim Hutchcraft
Claude Botts and Sharpie Shaw
Tom May and Dobie Leonard
Babe Johnson and Elbert Spicer
Clanney Johnson and Bill Nation

The day of the contest came and, after a big breakfast in Claude Botts' cabin, the teams departed into a strong northeast wind. The lake was full of mallards and canvasbacks, so a good hunt was expected.

The details of each team's hunt were not recalled by Mr. Lykin, but he does recall that he and Hutchcraft had a super hunt in the First Pocket area and had their limits by about 9:30. As they rowed out of the mouth of the Samburg ditch, they saw two boats crossing the open water ahead of them. Try as they would, they could not overtake them and the Jake Gibbs and Jack Hogg team won, with Babe Johnson and Elbert Spicer second.

It would sure be great to have ducks to enjoy like that again. These hunters and guides had the privilege of living and enjoying the greatest time of sport hunting ever.

John Lykin - great shot and promoter. We enjoyed many gunning days together.

DUCK BANDS IN THE FOG

I spent yesterday afternoon in the company of my oldest and one of my best friends at his surprise eightieth birthday party hosted by his daughter, Penny, at Boyette's Dining Room. As we spent time together we recalled many great times we have enjoyed with shotguns in hand.

One of those special days was in the mid-seventies and we were hunting from my first hunting camp, a sixty foot trailer on a small pie shaped lot on the east shore of Reelfoot Lake which I had purchased from Bim Barker in 1973. We were both shooting newly purchased Remington 1100 magnum shotguns and a special reload of 1 3/8 ounce of copper plated shot that traveled at over 1,300 feet per second similar to a load developed for Nash Buckingham by John Olin of Winchester Arms. We were hunting from the Lost Pond blind I purchased in 1971 from Parks Tigrett made famous by Elbert Spicer of market hunting fame.

It was early in the season and the lake had been frozen over for about a week. We were still running Reelfoot Lake type boats which made ice breaking easier because of the direct drive. The day of the hunt the ice was breaking up on a west wind and the Moultrie Field in front of the camp was partially open. As we left the bank we had a heavy fog, so we took a compass bearing which would take us across to the point of Willow Bar. Halfway across the open water we crossed Dobie Leonard's trail; he had gone out before us with his two men for the day. We hit a big stump and it shut off our motor. Before we could restart the motor we heard the roosting ducks quacking back in Rat Island Pocket. We headed in that direction rowing with our bow facing oars.

The fog had some breaks in it with day light fast approaching and we could see mallards swinging toward all the ducks on the water at the edge of the ice. Shooting time was upon us and as the ducks crossed overhead they were only twenty five or thirty yards high, "just right." Emery called the shot on a close pair and we folded them up as the sound of the shot flushed the mass roosting against the ice in the pocket. Then it was every man for himself. Pairs, singles and small groups crossed over us in the fog and when we had a break in the fog we took a quick shot. It was all over in a matter of minutes. As we rowed down the edge of the ice picking up our birds we noticed some of them were banded. Out of our eight mallards we had three bands, a first for both Emery and me.

As we motored on out to Lost Pond to check on our blind and decoys, we stopped to visit with Buddy Sedberry and Red Armstrong at the head of the Tom Johnson timber. We surely were proud of those bands and that quick limit. The blind was in fine shape but the decoys needed work, so for the next hour we straightened on the spread.

When we returned to camp I called the band numbers in to Washington and found all three mallards had been banded earlier in the year at the Reelfoot Refuge. I have killed around one hundred banded ducks in my hunting career but have only killed three in one day twice, both with Emery Burden. Once was on the lake in this story and the other on the Mississippi River outside the Hickman Harbor at our great hunting spot by the Crow Hole after a freeze-up late in the 1985 season.

As I write these stores I enjoy checking the calendars I have kept on each season the past forty years and remembering days past and the great hunts of times gone by.

Andrew Bowlin, Dr. "Chubby" Andrews, Russell Caldwell and Will Gurton.

The birds came all day.

THE GEESE CAME

When waterfowlers and gunners gather, the conversation always gets around to the greatest hunt or the one great hunt that stands out in their memory. Time takes me back to the last time the Canada geese migrated into our world. After 1992 and 1993, we wondered if it would ever happen again and the years started passing without any goose music. Mike Fraley was always faithful and optimistic. He said the year the cold weather and snow come to the prairies in December they would come, and it happened in the early winter of 2000.

The week was in December of 2000 and the Northern United States was locked into back to back blizzards and bone chilling cold for over two weeks. The time of the big week started on Sunday. We were hunting our pit on the north end of the Long Point Reelfoot Refuge with about fifty acres of frozen water; we were running our well around the clock trying to establish a five to ten acre hole of open water in case the birds did migrate. All Sunday afternoon we broke ice and shoved it under the thick ice around the hole and we cleaned up the decoys. The aerators were running and the well was pumping when the ducks started flying. We quit working about an hour before sunset and started hunting. The shoot was fast and we finished the day with a limit of those big northern red leg mallards and six geese, the big black feet we love to hunt.

Chubby Andrews came in for the hunt and we invited several other guests. Shawn Tankersley, Will Gurton, Andrew Bowlin, Doug Roth, Marvin Alexander and some of the other regulars were in readiness when Monday came and we were blessed with a nice duck shoot and several geese. The big bunches of migrators were not coming in yet, but it was still a wonderful time of birds, food and fellowship.

Then it was Tuesday, December 19th. Everyone was in the pit early and feathers and "goose doo" were all over the edge of the ice around the hole. The geese were everywhere; they had started during the night. As day broke in the east, lines of geese could be seen everywhere. The big "Dot" bunches were coming off the Hickman bluffs and off the river west of us. When they saw the open water sometimes they didn't beat a wing for over a mile as they coasted in. Other people came during the day to shoot when we got the word out the flight was on. Limits were filled on geese and we added almost a limit of ducks for everyone that hunted that day.

One of the bunches of geese was special; there were six in the bunch and they decoyed right in front of the pit amid clucks and growls on our faithful goose calls. When Rob called the shot, all six fell and when we retrieved them, four of the six were wearing leg bands. The rest of the story is that three of the four were within ten of the same number and were banded on the same day.

The flight lasted two more days. Our total for the five days was over 100 geese and five were banded. The ducks were equally impressive at over 200. It's been four years since that time. When I go to a memory that involves over a half century of waterfowling, I'll always remember this week with its special moments, wonderful friends and a special place to hunt.

WENDALL MORRIS

Wendall, a special and unique fellow with a big heart, can do it all. He is a guide, commercial fisherman and maker of sheet metal shell boxes, paddles, push poles and nets.

I have enjoyed a very special relationship with Wendall for over forty years. I can't think of all the things Wendall has given me over the years. No later than last week he gave me a new handmade net to refurbish the duck retrieving pole he had made for me years ago.

Wendall was head guide for the Broadbent Hunting Club (now White's Lake Refuge) in the 1940's and 1950's. He was an excellent shot on high ducks and he called them with a Two Finger Johnny Marsh call made for small men and women. He gave me the old call and his homemade shell box several years ago and from time to time I take them on the lake for old times sake.

He is still in pretty good health for his age and is the oldest living person who can really remember the good old days when the ducks shaded the sun as they flushed with a roar.

The Broadbent Club

GUIDES SCRIBES AND GUNNERS

GUIDES

Elbert Spicer

Carl Nance, Jerry Strader and Bill McClain

Jack Hogg

Jim Hutchcraft and "Sharpie" Shaw

The Fraley's - Doris, Chester and Mike
have all worked as guides on and around Reelfoot Lake.
Chester built the Tom Johnson timber blind used by the Fraley
family for years. Mike is my friend and is one of the hardest working
hunters I know. His mother, Doris, was the only lady guide on Reel-
foot and she guided sports that stayed at my Dad's small motel. She
called ducks with a small insert Johnny Marsh called a "Two Finger"
Marsh. Johnny was proud of this call and he checkered it for
her and gave it to her in 1950. She was a good shot and
loved Reelfoot Lake and the hunting environment.

Wayne Ervin - one of the early Reelfoot
guides helped my dad build his cabin and later
guided for him when he completed his motel in the 1950 era.

Pat Childress and Kenneth Norris

Tony Wigdor

"Chubby" Andrews and Charles Berry

Doug Roth, Jeff Shores (guide),
author, Larry Reddmann and "Chubby" Andrews

Louis Mikel - guide and photographer

J. E. Cochran and Sport

Harold Fowler - guided with "Sharpie" Shaw.

Photograph courtesy of Sharon Shaw Fowler Cunningham

Monroe Dean

Photograph courtesy of Sharon Shaw Fowler Cunningham

Garvin Powell, Foster Strader, Carl Nance and Hubert Woods.
The top guides on Upper Blue Basin in 1940's and 1950's.

Bud Morris - Reelfoot fisherman and boat dock manager
Photograph courtesy of Charlotte Hogg

SCRIBES

Dr. "Chubby" Andrews

Writers, Hunting Friends,

Nash Buckingham

Lifelong Companions and Top Gunners

Dr. "Chubby" Andrews, Wayne Capooth and author

Bobby Patterson (banker) and Spence Dupree (writer)

Dr. "Chubby" Andrews and Tom Makin

Harbert Alexander and Robert Kirkland

Rob Caldwell and John Taylor (writer)

Howard Harlan (historian and writer), Dr. "Chubby" Andrews and author

Donna Caldwell, Bonnie Cochran and Doris Lanzer

GUNNERS

Jake Gibbs - Obion County's premier gunner. Jake was a relative of General Gibbs, the founder of Union City, Tennessee. He told me he shot so much in the early 1900's that he used up the assets of the livery stable his dad left him. It was said that he shot quail so fast off a dog's point that the dog would dodge. My dad shot doves and trap with him in the 1930's. When Jake shot trap he always used a pump gun, and due to his bad flinching problem, his trap gun was equipped with a release trigger. He broke 98 X 100 targets to win the Senior Veteran Trophy at the Grand American in the 1950's. When I was a young man, I shot pigeons with Jake. He was still a great shot when he was in his eighties.

P. J. "Babe" Johnson - Remington Arms Shooter in the 1940's.
Owned a set of Glodo calls given to him by Charlie Thomas, Reelfoot Guide.

Grady Taylor - boat builder, teacher, duck call maker and dog trainer.
One of the best shots I ever hunted with. Special fellow and friend.

Chester Caldwell - businessman and hunter
My Dad

Harold

Our Sons

Robert, Harold and Russell (Author)

*Emery Burden and I killed over 40,000 crows up and
down the Mississippi River over the last 45 years. My Special Friend*

Buddy Sedberry and me
Buddy shot a three inch matted
rib Model 12 and was as good on high
ducks as anyone in this country. He blew a Loman
duck call and had a fifteen note high ball. It was great
to hunt with him in the 1960's and 1970's. He, Emery
Burden and I had many special days on the lake and river.

Guy Hogg in the Denton Hole

The Clendenin's

Dr. "Chubby" Andrews, Dolph Riggs and Dr. Richard Kies

Dr. "Chubby" Andrews, Phil Wynn, Brent Umberger and author

The author and Ron DeBerry

Duck call collectors

Pat Pitt on opening day in Arkansas

Christmas Day 1995

Harvey Pitt of DuQuoin, Illinois
The best decoy collector in my area.

Spence Dupree's pheasant shoot at Elmer Kahl's

Robert Caldwell, author, Larry Reddmann and Dr. "Chubby" Andrews

The author and Mike Fraley (One shoots them close.)

Billy Wayne Orr in Canada

Wendall Morris
Guide and commercial fisherman was locally famous
for making great push poles and paddles. He even made
special size boat seats, skiff oars and sheet metal shell boxes.
He made me a small net to catch baby turtles for my grandson, Matt.

Senator Roy Herron, Shawn Tankersley, Author,
Congressman John Tanner, Cotton Ivy, and Joe Hill.

Russell Smith and Tim Gibson after a pigeon shoot.

Stovall Kendrick and son Henry,
Dr. "Chubby" Andrews, Pat Pitt, Stephen Pitt and Patrick Pitt

Jeff Churan, Caleb Davis, III and author

*1957 was a very good year. I was a sophomore
in college. We had a 70 day duck season with a four
duck limit. I hunted and guided at every available opportunity.*

My Family

Russell Andrew Moore and Grandfather (Author)

FINISHING UP

In my life, I have had the privilege of journeying through a special place in time and space. Life on this earth is a time frame with a beginning and an end, and a lot of it is affected by the way one chooses to enjoy or live the time. Life is a three phase experience that starts with the preparation phase, then progresses to the happening of your journey with all the peaks and valleys a well lived life can bring on. The final phase is the time of remembrance when you look back on all the times you had and things you did along the way.

In my life, I think I was truly blessed; a wonderful family growing up, great friends and special times at all phases. My life's mate, Donna, has been a wonderful part of the journey as a mother, business partner and friend. My business career has been a forty-four year cycle of growth and tremendous change with special friends, customers and work sharers. My hobbies and collections have been both enriching and enjoyable. In 1959, when at University of Tennessee, I listed a lot of the things I wanted to accomplish in my journey (my life goals) and the good Lord saw me through them. I have lived in the best of times in a wonderful place (Reelfoot Lake) with the most wonderful people (my family and friends).

I am going to close this book with a few important things to consider. The most important thing in our lives is love, love of our Lord, love of our family and love of others. When you reach out to others you get your mind off yourself. Remember that life is a privilege, but to live it to the fullest is a choice.

As long as I have the memories of special friends, family and days afield on rivers and lakes, I can live over again the memories of times past and look forward to the future journey.

I close with an Irish blessing that means a lot to my family.

May the road rise to meet you
May the wind blow at your back
May the sun shine warmly on your face
May the rain fall softly on your fields
And until we meet again
May God hold you in the palm of his hand.

ACKNOWLEDGEMENTS

My special thanks to Robert E. Clendenin, Jr. , Dan Burch, Jr., Steve Orf, Chad DeBoard, Jim Johnson, Henry Lupton, Baughn Meredith, Albert Markham, Tennessee Wildlife Resources Museum and Archives, Sharon Shaw Fowler Cunningham, Craig Smith, Vern Sabin, Albert Gainer, Onis Strader, Charlotte Hogg, Jim Major, R. C. Owen and Donna Caldwell for photographic assistance and advice; Dr. "Chubby" Andrews for writing my foreword, the great photographs and encouragement he has provided for this project, and my world through the years. He is special. Thanks to Claire Dougherty for help with the design and pre-press management. A special thanks to Donna, the special lady in my life, without her a lot of things would not be done. She has gone over the book correcting, helping with suggestions and writing contributions that really put the book together as a joint effort as our life together has been. With the two of us working together, we get a more productive whole.

AUTHOR'S NOTES

While every effort is made by the author to present original information to the reader, I am grateful to have the following documents and publications as reference source materials: Reelfoot - An Earthquake Lake by Wilbur A. Nelson; National Geographic Magazine, January 1924; David Crockett, Autobiography, 1891; History of Reelfoot Lake, by W. E. Lowe, 1930; The History of the Reelfoot Lake Region, by C. C. Humphreys, 1938; Obion County History, Reelfoot Lake, 1925; The New Madrid Earthquake of 1811-1812 by James Penick, Jr., 1976; Tennessee Historical Quarterly, Fall 1973; Reelfoot Lake State Park, by Blanche G. Peacock; Union City Daily Messenger; Union City Commercial, 1903; The New Madrid Quake by Juanita Clifton; Nash Buckingham, Beaver Dam and Other Hunting Tales by Dr. W. F. "Chubby" Andrews; Ole Miss by Nash Buckingham.

Photograph by Craig Smith